3 Months to Live

Andy Furman

Front Cover Artwork Designed by

Julie Furman

Acknowledgements

This book is written with special thanks and gratitude to the following people who have helped shape and direct my life immensely.

To my best friend Julie, for her love, compassion, and humility. Her encouraging and gentle spirit as a wife, mom, grandmother, friend, and follower of Christ has been evident in all of her relationships and endeavors. The commitment and consistency of her prayer life has been inspirational and an example to emulate. I am so thankful that God has allowed me to do life together with you and I look forward to what the future holds for us, while continuing to grow closer to you through it all.

Proverbs 31:10, 11, 26, 30, 31
Who can find a virtuous and capable wife? She is more precious than rubies. Her husband can trust her, and she will greatly enrich his life. When she speaks, her words are wise, and she gives instructions with kindness. Charm is deceptive, and beauty does not last; but a woman who fears the Lord will be greatly praised. Reward her for all she has done. Let her deeds publicly declare her praise.

To my dad, Courtney Furman. As a teacher and pastor for 50 years I believe his passion was to glorify God, to help people discover who God was and how He could impact their lives, and then to guide them as they grew in their relationship with Christ. As a dad, that was his passion as well, and I will be eternally grateful for the guidance and example he provided. His insight and wisdom over the years was greatly appreciated and I hope he knew how much I valued it. He was also an exceptionally generous man, giving of his time and resources as any need arose.

Matthew 6:19-21
"Don't store up treasures here on earth, where moths eat them and rust destroys them, and where thieves break in and steal. Store your treasures in heaven, where moths and rust cannot destroy, and thieves do not break in and steal. Wherever your treasure is, there the desires of your heart will be also."

To my youth pastor and friend, Dwight Wilkins. His dedication to invest in our lives as teenagers was pivotal as we navigated through those formative years. Through his friendship, instruction, and witness, he planted seeds that created a hunger to grow in my relationship with Christ. Dwight helped us establish a firm foundation in our faith that has not been shaken. I admire your continued service and obedience to follow God's leading.

2 Timothy 2:15
Work hard so you can present yourself to God and receive his approval. Be a good worker, one who does not need to be ashamed and who correctly explains the word of truth.

To my friend Kenny Lewis, whose pastoral influence early in our marriage led Julie and I to a renewed commitment to our faith and service. His bold teachings and emphasis on witnessing and discipleship challenged us to focus our perspective and energies on eternal relationships. We were also blessed and inspired by Connie and Kenny's marriage and parenting examples during that time and through the years.

Acts 20:24
But my life is worth nothing to me unless I use it for finishing the work assigned me by the Lord Jesus - the work of telling others the Good News about the wonderful grace of God.

And to so many men and women who have impacted our lives over the years through mentorship, friendship, encouragement, and their examples of Christ. We have been blessed and are thankful to be a part of such a wonderful body of believers.

1 Corinthians 12:12, 18
The human body has many parts, but the many parts make up one whole body. So it is with the body of Christ. But our bodies have many parts, and God has put each part just where he wants it.

Finally, to my children and grandchildren with whom God has abundantly filled our quiver! I cherish the memories and milestones that we have shared and look forward to many more.

My prayer for you is that you will embrace the plan that God has for your life and to seek and follow His will. To love what He loves, and for His desires to be the desires of your heart.

Psalms 127:3-5 & 37:4
Children are a gift from the Lord; they are a reward from him. Children born to a young man are like arrows in a warrior's hands. How joyful is the man whose quiver is full of them! He will not be put to shame when he confronts his accusers at the city gates. Take delight in the Lord, and he will give you your heart's desires.

3 Months to Live

Perspective, Priorities & Purpose

Where there is no vision, the people perish: But he that keepeth the law, happy is he. Proverbs 29:18 KJV

A heavy sense of dread and anxiety engulfed the waiting room in anticipation of hearing the severity of the test results. Time ticked slowly, heightening the tension until the oncologist finally entered with the sobering news. The words were hard to fathom. The prognosis was devastating. Inoperable . . . . . Untreatable . . . . . At best, 3 months to live.

As the shock and sadness of your mortality begins to set in, your mind wanders to those closest to you. How will this affect them and how will they carry on without you? What can you do to help them prepare for after you are gone?

In your reflections you consider how you have lived your life and what impact you have had. Your thoughts drift to the investments you have made and the legacy you will leave behind. Questions race through your mind. What will I do with these last 3 months? Whom will I spend them with? What should I pursue? How can I make a difference with the time that I have left?

The reality is that each of us has a certain amount of time remaining on this earth and none of us know how much longer it will be. James reminds us of the uncertainty and brevity of our existence. *James 4:14 How do you know what your life will be like tomorrow? Your life is like the morning fog - it's here a little while, then it's gone.* Whether you have 3 months or 70 years remaining, the question we all need to ask is the same. **Am I living the life that God intended for me to live?**

As I look back on my life, I have been very fortunate and blessed in countless ways. I have a wonderful family and many amazing friendships, have had enjoyable and fulfilling work opportunities, and have been a part of numerous genuine church fellowships. I have witnessed God's guidance and continued provisions and when faced with trials and hardships, his presence has always sustained and his faithfulness has been new every morning.

Through the difficulties and challenges of 2020, God's Spirit has been a steadying force and comfort. As job uncertainties and other concerns have lingered, his word has reassured me of who is in control, and has narrowed my focus to trust his will and plan for the rest of my life. One of my favorite passages is *Proverbs 3:5, 6 Trust in the Lord with all your heart, do not depend on your own understanding. Seek his will in all you do, and he will show you which path to take.* He desires to direct each of our paths. We simply need to trust his wisdom and accept his leadership.

In processing these thoughts I have sensed God's prompting to write this book. I believe that he is sending believers a message through the circumstances of this past year to examine our lives and priorities. Are we focused on what is important to him and what is eternal? Are we being a light to a lost world and living our lives accordingly? Are we maturing in our faith? Is there evidence of love, joy, peace, patience, kindness, goodness, faithfulness, gentleness and self-control? Are we sharing his message of salvation? **Is there an urgency to the way we are spending the days that he has appointed for us, whether they be weeks or decades?** Over these past few months I have been contemplating and evaluating my priorities, my relationship with Him and with those in my life, my level of obedience, witness, and growth.

As this is my first venture into writing and since I am a bottom line person, the message will be direct, to the point, and ideally will result in a quick, yet valuable read. I share these words of encouragement and insight from my heart and life's experiences in order to help as you strive to discover and follow God's desire for your life. I am not an expert in any of these areas, but he is! His word is the truth and provides all of the guidance and answers that we will ever need. As his commands are eternal, these pages will be filled with Scriptural references - His words of wisdom that are associated with each topic. *Hebrews 13:8, 9 Jesus Christ is the same yesterday, today, and forever. So do not be attracted by strange, new ideas. Your strength comes from God's grace, not from rules about food, which don't help those who follow them.*

Throughout each chapter I have included a few questions for you to ponder as well as some practical applications to assist in your walk, as you are led. If any of these questions or topics hit close to home, I strongly encourage you not to ignore or avoid them. As I have read and studied over the years, I have experienced the Holy Spirit's instructions, convictions, and warnings. The times that I have ignored his prodding have brought painful lessons, disappointment, and sadness. My intention is not to dredge up the past but to acknowledge that we all mourn lost opportunities and have regrets. However, those do not have to define our future. Paul urges us to press on in *Philippians 3:13, 14 No, dear brothers and sisters, I have not achieved it, but I focus on this one thing: Forgetting the past and looking forward to what lies ahead, I PRESS ON to reach the end of the race and receive the heavenly prize for which God, through Christ Jesus, is calling us.*

Satan delights in limiting our witness and slowing our spiritual growth by using the guilt and shame of past failures to make us question our worth and potential. We must remember that we have been washed in the Blood of Jesus and instructed to press on, to continue to run the race that he has set before us, and that his desire is for us to live a victorious life, believing that we can do all things through Christ who strengthens us. Living in his power and following his plan is his calling for each of us, as long as we are alive. Whether you are a teenager/young adult, a married couple with children, an active retiree, or a senior in your final chapter, God's exhortation for all of us is to keep running that race, to not grow weary, and to fix our eyes on Jesus.

Hebrews 12:1-3 Therefore, since we are surrounded by such a huge cloud of witnesses to the life of faith, let us strip off every weight that slows us down, especially the sin that so easily trips us up. And let us run with endurance the race God has set before us. We do this by keeping our eyes on Jesus, the champion who initiates and perfects our faith. Because of the joy awaiting him, he endured the cross, disregarding its shame. Now he is seated in the place of honor beside God's throne. Think of all the hostility he endured from sinful people; then you won't become weary and give up.

As we focus our **perspective** on eternity, God's Word, and His people, we will **prioritize** our days accordingly. The talents, passions, and desires that he has gifted to us, when aligned with his plan, will allow us to fulfill that **purpose** which he has called us to pursue, for His Glory. *Jeremiah 29:11 "For I know the plans I have for you," says the Lord. "They are plans for good and not for disaster, to give you a future and a hope."*

My prayer is that as you read through these chapters and meditate on **His words**, you will ask God to reveal his desire for you in each area of your life, and that you will embrace his leading, being able to testify as Paul did in *2 Timothy 4:7 I have fought the good fight, I have finished the race, and I have remained faithful!*

If you have made it this far and are a bit confused or unfamiliar with this subject, let me ask you a question. Have you ever accepted Jesus Christ as your personal Savior and surrendered the Lordship of your life over to him? That is the most important decision that anyone will make during their life - it will affect their experience here on earth, as well as determine where they will spend eternity.

This book is intended to encourage and strengthen Christians in their relationship with, and obedience to, God. Before we continue though, I would like to share God's plan for your salvation. As you read this, I pray that the Holy Spirit would open your hearts to this message and that you would receive it and begin your new life in Christ.

In Genesis, the first book of the Bible, God tells us that he created the heavens and the earth and all that was in it. The acknowledgement and belief that he is our Creator and the designer of all things is the starting point to having a relationship with him. Throughout history many people wrote and prophesied about a coming Messiah, specifically pertaining to numerous details including his lineage, birth place, ministry, death, and resurrection. All of these were fulfilled in the person of Jesus Christ when he came to earth. I mention this to emphasize that belief in Jesus is not just following a blind faith or having to choose between his message as opposed to a big bang concept, evolution, or a philosophy that there is no god.

Mathematics and science professor Peter Stoner has made the statement "that the chances of just 8 of these prophecies coming true in one person are 1 in 100,000,000,000,000,000."[1]

If you can accept that there is One God, a literal heaven or hell final destination for all of us, and that the Biblical writings were inspired by God, then you have been given a very clear and specific plan for your salvation.

- God loves you and wants to have a relationship with you. That is why you were created. *John 3:16   "For this is how God loved the world: He gave his one and only Son, so that everyone who believes in him will not perish but have eternal life."*

- Sin has separated you from God because he is holy and sinless. We have all sinned; it doesn't matter how many times or how bad we think our sin is. One sin keeps you from a relationship with him. It separates you now and for eternity. *Romans 3:23   For everyone has sinned; we all fall short of God's glorious standard.*

- God loved you so much that he sent his own son, Jesus, to be the payment for your sin so that you could enter into that relationship with him. No sin is too big, no one is hopeless. He offers this gift to everyone. *Romans 5:8 But God showed his great love for us by sending Christ to die for us while we were still sinners. Romans 6:23 For the wages of sin is death, but the free gift of God is eternal life through Christ Jesus our Lord.*

- If you put your belief and trust in him and accept his gift of salvation, you will be saved. *Romans 10:9, 10 If you openly declare that Jesus is Lord and believe in your heart that God raised him from the dead, you will be saved. For it is by believing in your heart that you are made right with God, and it is by openly declaring your faith that you are saved.   Romans 10:13 For "Everyone who calls on the name of the Lord will be saved."*

- Jesus told us that He is the only way. *John 14:6 Jesus told him, "I am the way, the truth, and the life. No one can come to the Father except through me."*

By simply praying and admitting that you have sinned, asking for forgiveness, thanking God for the gift of Jesus who paid the penalty for your sin, accepting that gift by letting Jesus take over your life, and then giving him the control as you live according to his plan, you will be saved.

When you do that, the Holy Spirit will enter your life and provide guidance, direction, and insights as you ask for wisdom and begin to learn what God has planned for you. Reading the Bible, praying, and getting involved with other Christians is vital in helping you develop this relationship and growing closer to him. As with anything new, there can be confusion and uncertainty as you begin this journey. Please know that when you make this decision I would love to help you in any way I can, assisting in finding a church near you, answering questions, praying for you, or whatever is needed. My contact email is:

furmanandy1@gmail.com

You are now a new creation in Christ, you have his Spirit to lead you, and you will dwell in the house of the Lord forever! The lyrics in this song of surrender by Judson Van DeVenter express the joys of what your newfound focus and identity will involve.

> "All to Jesus I surrender, all to him I freely give. I will ever love and trust him, in his presence daily live.
>
> All to Jesus I surrender, humbly at his feet I bow. Worldly pleasures all forsaken, take me Jesus, take me now.
>
> All to Jesus I surrender, Make me Savior wholly thine. May thy Holy Spirit fill me, may I know thy power divine.
>
> I surrender all; I surrender all. All to thee my blessed Savior, **I surrender ALL**."

"In the same way, there is joy in the presence of God's angels when even one sinner repents." Luke 15:10

It All Begins with God

Jesus replied "You must love the Lord your God with all your heart, all your soul, and all your mind. This is the first and greatest commandment." Matthew 22:37, 38

This first commandment succinctly sums up what our top priority as a follower of Christ should be – **to love God with all of our heart, soul, and mind**. Pretty cut and dried. Nothing too theologically deep in that statement or hard to understand. And once we have mastered that, every other area of our life will be lined up with his plan!

Unfortunately, obedience to this command is much easier said than done and many times we fall short. However, that should not keep us from striving towards this goal each day. God sees the battles we face and understands that he is the only one who can lead us to victory. He exhorts us to love him with all of our heart – every desire and emotion; with all our soul – our will and actions; and with our entire mind – each thought and spoken word. He knows that as we press on, continue to run the race and persevere, we are being conformed to his image and bringing glory to his name in all of our pursuits.

God is our creator, the author of all life, the Alpha and Omega. *Colossians 1:16 For through him God created everything in the heavenly realms and on earth. He made the things we can see and the things we can't see - such as thrones, kingdoms, rulers, and authorities in the unseen world. Everything was created through him and for him.* He is omniscient, omnipotent, and omnipresent – infinite attributes that our finite minds have difficulty grasping. As he formed the world and all that is in it, he has also created you with a specific plan in mind for your life.

He intended to have a personal relationship with you and to enjoy daily fellowship with you. His desire is to love, guide and bless you so that you will follow his example, embrace him in return, and be emboldened to share his love with those he brings into your life. That is the second commandment, *Matthew 22:39 "A second is equally important: Love your neighbor as yourself."*

As Christians we have been taught that God should be the most important thing in our life. Most of us recognize this and it is our go to answer, an automatic response. "Of course God is my # 1 priority." I have used that line for 45 years and there have been seasons where it was an accurate assessment of my relationship with him – investing time, seeking and following his will, developing an intimate and personal connection. There have been other periods where my commitment was less than enthusiastic and I lacked the desire to pursue his direction and leading, resulting in a distant and fruitless stage. I have found that as I live out this first commandment faithfully, it is reflected in, and impacts every area of my life and sphere of influence.

In the book of Matthew, Jesus uses a parable of a farmer sowing his seed to point out the importance of our continued growth and to help us evaluate our level of commitment to him. *Matthew 13:3-9 He told many stories in the form of parables, such as this one: "Listen! A farmer went out to plant some seeds. As he scattered them across his field, some seeds fell on a footpath, and the birds came and ate them. Other seeds fell on shallow soil with underlying rock. The seeds sprouted quickly because the soil was shallow. But the plants soon wilted under the hot sun, and since they didn't have deep roots, they died. Other seeds fell among thorns that grew up and choked out the tender plants. Still other seeds fell on fertile soil, and they produced a crop that was thirty, sixty, and even a hundred times as much as had been planted! Anyone with ears to hear should listen and understand."*

Jesus continued with the interpretation. *Matthew 13:18-23 "Now listen to the explanation of the parable about the farmer planting seeds: The seed that fell on the footpath represents those who hear the message about the Kingdom and don't understand it. Then the evil one comes and snatches away the seed that was planted in their hearts. The seed on the rocky soil represents those who hear the message and immediately receive it with joy. But since they don't have deep roots, they don't last long. They fall away as soon as they have problems or are persecuted for believing God's word. The seed that fell among the thorns represents those who hear God's word, but all too quickly the message is crowded out by the worries of this life and the lure of wealth, so no fruit is produced. The seed that fell on good soil represents those who truly hear and understand God's word and produce a harvest of thirty, sixty, or even a hundred times as much as had been planted!"*

What stage of growth is your seed at presently along this path? Have you heard his calling but never received it? Maybe you have made a profession of faith but have not developed the relationship past that point. Are you lost in the weeds of life, having forgotten your first love? Or are you flourishing and producing a bumper crop? As appealing as the Gospel message is and our desire is to move forward in our growth with childlike faith, Satan is constantly lurking, scheming, and attempting to deceive us and destroy our relationship with God. This path is our life long journey and wherever you are, whatever the state of your current relationship is, know that he will never leave or forsake you. If you have wandered off the path and are stuck in the thorns, he is waiting and longing for your return. And if you are planted in good soil then continue to seek and grow, thanking him for what he is accomplishing through you, until your days on this earth come to an end. *John 15:5 "Yes, I am the vine; you are the branches. Those who remain in me, and I in them, will produce much fruit. For apart from me you can do nothing."*

In his book "Knowing God"[2] J. I. Packer discusses 4 evidences in believers of a growing spiritual maturity.

- Those who know God have great **energy** for God.
- Those who know God have great **thoughts** of God.
- Those who know God show great **boldness** for God.
- Those who know God have great **contentment** in God.

In an honest evaluation of your daily routine and practices, how do you invest your energy and time? Towards what are your thoughts most often directed? Where does boldness display itself in your life? What brings you true contentment and peace?

Paul spoke of this in his letter to the *Philippians 4:4-9 Always be full of joy in the Lord. I say it again - rejoice! Let everyone see that you are considerate in all you do. Remember, the Lord is coming soon. Don't worry about anything; instead, pray about everything. Tell God what you need, and thank him for what he has done. Then you will experience God's peace, which exceeds anything we can understand. His peace will guard your hearts and minds as you live in Christ Jesus. And now, dear brothers and sisters, one final thing. Fix your thoughts on what is true, and honorable, and right, and pure, and lovely, and admirable. Think about things that are excellent and worthy of praise.* Keep putting into practice all you learned and received from me - *everything you heard from me and saw me doing. Then the God of peace will be with you.* What a promise! As we rejoice in the Lord always, give our all continually to him, and dwell on what is excellent and worthy of praise, God's peace will be with us. And the resulting life we lead will be filled with great energy for him, great thoughts of him, great boldness for him, and great contentment in him.

Any relationship that you wish to develop requires an investment of time and effort. I believe there are five key areas to address in order for us to continually be growing closer to God.

- We must read and study his word
- Spend time with him in prayer
- Worship him with others
- Regularly fellowship with his believers
- Follow his Great Commission

As physical nourishment is required on a daily basis in order to develop and maintain our health, these five areas – instruction, communication, praise, encouragement and outreach are necessary on a daily basis also, to give us the spiritual nourishment which is vital for our Christian development and growth. There are no magic formulas or special rituals to follow in these areas but there are many resources and fellow believers available to aid in your studying of the Bible, developing your prayer life, helping you get plugged into a solid group of believers, and sharing your faith. My experience has been that when you ask the Holy Spirit for insight to guide and direct your growth, he will provide wisdom and discernment in every area of your life.

Studying the Bible gives you God's perspective on his plan and direction for your life. *Joshua 1:8 Study this Book of Instruction continually. Meditate on it day and night so you will be sure to obey everything written in it. Only then will you* *prosper and succeed in all you do.* Memorizing verses equips you for situations that occur throughout each day and provides strength and clarity that is contrary to the world's views. *Psalms 119:11 I have hidden your word in my heart, that I might not sin against you.*

God desires daily conversations with his people, to praise and thank him for all he has done, to confess our sins and ask for his forgiveness, and to bring our requests before him. This should be on a regular basis, even throughout the day, not just when a crisis occurs or a great need arises in our life. An acronym that has been helpful in my prayer life is **ACTS**.

- **A**doration   Acknowledging his attributes, who he is, what he has created, and how he reigns above all.
- **C**onfession   Repentance and seeking forgiveness for sins that he brings to mind that I've committed and for victory in any area that I might face that day.
- **T**hanksgiving   Recognizing and expressing appreciation for all he does and the blessings he has given.
- **S**upplication   Bringing concerns and requests to him, and asking him to intercede for any needs of others.

I have found that singing or reading praise songs and old hymns enhances my adoration experience. I learned this from an early age by watching the example of my dad as he appreciated the beauty, power, and truths that proclaimed the Word of God through music. Keeping a journal of prayer requests and the dates and outcomes of the way God has answered them increases our faith and reaffirms how he is continually working in our lives. Beginning your day with him prepares you for anything that will occur and reminds you of what is important and who is watching over all that you will encounter. *Mark 1:35 Before daybreak the next morning, Jesus got up and went out to an isolated place to pray. Psalms 37:7 Be still in the presence of the Lord, and wait patiently for him to act. Do not worry about evil people who prosper or fret about their wicked schemes.*

We were created to have fellowship with and to worship God Almighty. He alone is worthy of our adulation. We hear this in the vision of his throne in heaven with the 4 living creatures repeating "Holy, Holy, Holy is the Lord God Almighty. Who was, and is, and is to come." We see the 24 elders fall before him and worship the one who lives forever.

Revelation 4:11 KJV "Thou art worthy, O Lord, to receive glory and honour and power: for thou hast created all things, and for thy pleasure they are and were created." As we worship we begin to see a glimpse of what is to come and that creates a hunger and thirst to be in his presence. *Psalm 63:1 KJV O God, thou art My God; early will I seek thee: My soul thirsteth for thee, my flesh longeth for thee in a dry and thirsty land, where no water is.*

The early church and believers had an urgency to their fellowship. They were few in number, new to this faith, suffering persecution, and yet they did not neglect meeting together regularly to pray, study, eat, and minister to each other's needs. We are instructed as well to encourage one another, share our talents and resources, and to stir up one another to love and to do good works. *Philippians 2:1-4 Is there any encouragement from belonging to Christ? Any comfort from his love? Any fellowship together in the Spirit? Are your hearts tender and compassionate? Then make me truly happy by agreeing wholeheartedly with each other, loving one another, and working together with one mind and purpose. Don't be selfish; don't try to impress others. Be humble, thinking of others as better than yourselves. Don't look out only for your own interests, but take an interest in others, too.* Sadly, the emptiness, loneliness, despair, and lack of contentment experienced by too many has resulted from their inward focus, rather than relying on God's plan for us to be engaged in fellowship and helping those in need. *Hebrews 10:25 And let us not neglect our meeting together, as some people do, but encourage one another, especially now that the day of his return is drawing near.*

As a disciple of Christ we are his ambassadors, sent into the world to represent him and to give witness to what he has done.

2 Corinthians 5:20   So we are Christ's ambassadors; God is making his appeal through us. We speak for Christ when we plead, "Come back to God!" We must testify to the work he has accomplished in our lives and use the gifts he has given us to share his message and to train up those he brings across our path.

We must strive to be obedient in each of these areas as God has called us to grow our faith into its full maturity.

Colossians 2:6,7   And now, just as you accepted Christ Jesus as your Lord, you must continue to follow him. Let your roots grow down into him, and let your lives be built on him. Then your faith will grow strong in the truth you were taught, and you will overflow with thankfulness.

Lyrics from the popular song 'Trust and Obey' by John Sammis, sum up this transformation that takes place.

> "When we walk with the Lord in the light of his word, what a glory he sheds on our way!
>
> While we do his good will, he abides with us still, and with all who will trust and obey.
>
> Then in fellowship sweet, we will sit at his feet, or we'll walk by his side in the way.
>
> What he says we will do, where he sends we will go, never fear, only trust and obey."

As you continue to trust and obey, God will direct your **heart** towards his desires, your **will** towards his plan, and your **mind** towards his kingdom. He knows you better than you know yourself, nothing is hidden from his sight, and he wants to complete the good work that he has started in you!   *Hebrews 4:12, 13   For the word of God is alive and powerful. It is sharper than the sharpest two-edged sword, cutting between soul and spirit, between joint and marrow. It exposes our innermost thoughts and desires. Nothing in all creation is hidden from God. Everything is naked and exposed before his eyes, and he is the one to whom we are accountable.*

I love this hymn by Stuart Townend and Keith Getty, "In Christ Alone."[3] It has always been a powerful reminder of who God is and who we are in him. I get chills every time it is sung, and it perfectly reinforces the title of this chapter: **It all Begins with God**.

> "In Christ alone my hope is found, He is my light, my strength, my song. This Cornerstone, this solid Ground, Firm through the fiercest drought and storm,
>
> What heights of love, what depths of peace, When fears are stilled, when strivings cease. My Comforter, my All in All, Here in the love of Christ I stand.
>
> In Christ alone! – who took on flesh, Fullness of God in helpless babe. This gift of love and righteousness, Scorned by the ones He came to save.
>
> Till on that cross as Jesus died, The wrath of God was satisfied. For every sin on Him was laid, Here in the death of Christ I live.
>
> There in the ground His body lay, Light of the world by darkness slain: Then bursting forth in glorious day, Up from the grave He rose again.
>
> And as He stands in victory, Sin's curse has lost its grip on me, For I am His and He is mine, Bought with the precious blood of Christ.
>
> No guilt in life, no fear in death, This is the power of Christ in me. From life's first cry to final breath, Jesus commands my destiny.
>
> No power of hell, no scheme of man, Can ever pluck me from His hand. Till He returns or calls me home, Here in the power of Christ I'll stand."

And whatever you do or say, do it as a representative of the Lord Jesus, giving thanks through him to God the Father. Colossians 3:17

Loving My Spouse as Christ Loves His Church

And further, submit to one another out of reverence for Christ.
For wives, this means submit to your husbands as to the Lord.
For husbands, this means love your wives, just as Christ loved
the church. Ephesians 5:21, 22, 25

God's love for us and his gift of salvation, which allows us to enter into a relationship with him, is the example he established for us to imitate in our marriage. The attributes below that he exhibits toward his church, are designed to be the perfect model of the love that we should display toward our spouse.

- **Selfless**   Concerned more with the needs and wishes of others than oneself
- **Unconditional** Absolute, limitless, without end.
- **Permanent**   Existing perpetually, everlasting, without significant change

As we reflect on what Christ has sacrificed for us, our desire to love, serve, and honor our spouse flows from the respect and thankfulness that we have for the manner in which God first loved us.

A common view in our world when it comes to marriage is that it is a 50-50 proposition. We split up the chores, tasks, and responsibilities as equally as possible, choosing those that best fit our skill sets or those which we find less tedious.   Occasionally on a good day, we are willing to go above and beyond and give a 60% effort if there are extenuating circumstances that might dictate it! We think of others and lend a helpful hand as long as it is convenient or does not require too much sacrifice on our part. To deny our own desires is not normal behavior, we are sinful by nature and wired to think of ourselves first. Our society promotes an "It's all about ME" philosophy, and the attitude that "You need to take care of yourself first." We have a tendency to compare how we are loved and treated and will offer our love in return as long as we perceive that it is deserved or being reciprocated. There is often a ledger kept of slights and offenses that influence our affections and efforts. And tragically, we are seeing less permanence and levels of commitment, with marriages ending as emotions fluctuate, expectations go unmet, and the "feelings" of love fade.

A truly selfless attitude that loves unconditionally and will never cease, can only be cultivated through our relationship with Christ. This is known as Agape love, not a feeling or an emotion but love in the form of an action, originating from God's unconditional love for us. I Corinthians 13 is famously referred to as the "Love Chapter" and portions of it are recited at many weddings. Its emphasis is on the specific characteristics of Christ's love in action, how they are manifested in our daily lives, and how expressions of other qualities mean nothing if they are not rooted in love. If you can speak in tongues, have the gift of prophecy, use your incredible faith to move mountains, or give all you have to the poor but do not love others, you are nothing. You gain nothing. They are worthless abilities even if they appear to be worthwhile.

To help emphasize the impact and scope of God's love for us as described in verses 4 through 8, it was suggested to me years ago to substitute Christ for the word love. *I Corinthians 13:4-8 Christ is patient, Christ is kind, Christ is not jealous, Christ does not boast, Christ is not proud. Christ is not rude, Christ does not demand his own way, Christ is not irritable, Christ keeps no record of wrongs. Christ does not rejoice in injustice but Christ rejoices with the truth. Christ always protects, Christ always trusts, Christ always hopes, and Christ always perseveres. Christ never fails.* Are these characteristics displayed in your communication, expectations, beliefs, and attitudes with your spouse?

- Patient – Accepts or tolerates delay, problems, or suffering without becoming annoyed or anxious.
- Kind – Has a well-meaning disposition; considerate, helpful.
- Is not Jealous – Does not feel resentful or discontented by another's qualities or possessions.
- Does not Boast, is not Proud – Does not speak with deep pleasure and self-satisfaction about one's achievements, possessions, or abilities.
- Is not Rude - impolite or ill-mannered.
- Does not Demand its own way – Is not concerned for one's own welfare and interests before those of others.
- Is not Irritable – Is not easily annoyed, testy, upset, or offended.

- Keeps no Record of Wrongs – Is not easily provoked or resentful. Thinks no evil.
- Rejoices with the Truth – Dwells on that which is true in accordance with fact and reality. God and His Word.
- Protects – Keep safe from harm or injury.
- Trusts – Believes in the reliability, truth, ability, and strength of another.
- Hopes – Has expectations and desires for a certain thing to happen.
- Perseveres – Continues to strive to achieve despite difficulties, failures or opposition; remains steadfast.
- Never Fails – God's love – Agape love, is Selfless, Unconditional and Eternal.

As you contemplate the daily interactions with your spouse, how is this passage being manifested? Developing a Godly and fulfilling relationship is what he desires and intended for our marriages, and serves as a witness to others of his love and commitment to his people. When relying on your own strength, your selfish and sinful nature will win the battle more often than not, hindering your growth in him and as a couple. However, when your love is centered in Christ, a cord of three strands is not easily broken.

Ecclesiastes 4:9-12 KJV Two are better than one; because they have a good reward for their labour. For if they fall, the one will lift up his fellow: but woe to him that is alone when he falleth; for he hath not another to help him up. Again, if two lie together, then they have heat: but how can one be warm alone? And if one prevail against him, two shall withstand him; and a threefold cord is not quickly broken.

Just as in our relationship with God, our marriage will only reach its pinnacle by committing our time and efforts to that end. In our early years I came across a quote with this simple, yet profound message. **"What you truly love you will make time for."** I had Julie make a plaque with that written on it for my office, to be a reminder of where my focus should lie. After God, our spouse should be our most important priority and who we are most devoted to. It does not matter what season of life you are in – whether raising children, establishing a business, leading a ministry, or enjoying retirement - nurturing this relationship has to come first.

Does your spouse know that they are more important to you than your children, grandchildren, job, hobbies, friends, or parents? How is the majority of your time spent each day? What are your efforts and energies most often directed towards? What do you "truly love" and consistently "make time for"? Does your husband know that he is respected, admired and his efforts are greatly appreciated? Does your wife feel affirmed and cherished, experiencing your affection, knowing you desire her above all else?

Whether you are approaching the twilight of your life or have many years of wedded bliss remaining, how would you evaluate the current health of your relationship and your role in it? Any changes or new investments that might be required in order to continue to experience growth or potentially revive your relationship are worth whatever effort it will take, and will result in the marriage that God has planned for you. He desires to give both of you direction and is capable of helping you to forgive, to heal any wound, and to stir every heart, longing for your union to prosper and flourish. *1 Peter 4:8 Most important of all, continue to show deep love for each other, for love covers a multitude of sins.*

Julie and I have witnessed God's grace and His power of reconciliation in our marriage. We know the despair, trauma, guilt and pain of going through a separation and divorce firsthand. We have also been able to experience the blessings of being reunited, thankful for God's hand in leading us back together. Remember, the One who has set the stars in the skies, formed the highest mountains, carved out the deepest oceans, and formed you and me in his image - from dust and a rib - it is He who is able to breathe life into any marriage. Even one where there appears to be no hope. **He is our Hope**.

Isaiah 40:25-31 KJV "To whom then will ye liken me, or shall I be equal?" saith the Holy One. Lift up your eyes on high, and behold who hath created these things, that bringeth out their host by number: he calleth them all by names by the greatness of his might, for that he is strong in power; not one faileth. Why sayest thou, O Jacob, and speakest, O Israel, My way is hid from the LORD, and my judgment is passed over from my God? Hast thou not known? Hast thou not heard, that the everlasting God, the LORD, the Creator of the ends of the earth, fainteth not, neither is weary? There is no searching of his understanding. He giveth power to the faint; and to them that have no might he increaseth strength. Even the youths shall faint and be weary, and the young men shall utterly fall: **but they that wait upon the LORD shall renew their strength;** *they shall mount up with wings as eagles; they shall run, and not be weary; and they shall walk, and not faint."*

Men, we are directed by God to be the spiritual leaders in our homes. We should not be intimidated by this responsibility or question our abilities or qualifications as we are to imitate the example of servant leadership modeled for us by Christ. *Ephesians 5:25 For husbands, this means love your wives, just as Christ loved the church.* This does not mean that the husband is more important to God or that wives are not as spiritual, as he clearly loves all of us the same and sees us as his children with no favorites. We are reminded in *Galatians 3:28 There is no longer Jew or Gentile, slave or free, male and female. For you are all one in Christ Jesus.* It is just a simple fact that a marriage, family, team, or organization needs a leader in order to thrive and be successful and God has assigned that role to the husbands. *Colossians 3:18, 19 Wives, submit to your husbands, as is fitting for those who belong to the Lord. Husbands, love your wives and never treat them harshly.*

I have never met anyone who was not willing or excited to follow the leadership of someone who exhibited the attributes described in I Corinthians 13. Someone who is Patient. Kind. Does not Envy. Does not Boast. Is not Proud. Is not Rude. Does not Demand his own way. Is not easily Irritated. Keeps no record of Wrongs. Rejoices in the Truth. Hopes. Perseveres. Never Fails. As you lead your wife in a selfless and unconditional manner, having assured her of your permanent commitment to her, displaying Christ like love for her, seeking and valuing her insights, wisdom, and assistance, she will embrace your leadership and be the helpmate that God designed her to be. *Genesis 2:18 KJV And the LORD God said "It is not good that the man should be alone; I will make him a help meet for him."*

It is no accident or random assignment that the term helpmate was given for this purpose. In Hebrew the word help mate, or help meet is derived from two words, Ezer Kenegdo.

Depending on the pronunciation, Ezer means (1) to save or rescue; (2) to be strong. This term is used many times throughout the Old Testament in reference to God as their helper and savior, and is also used in Genesis referring to His creation of the suitable helper for Adam. Kenegdo is translated as; corresponding to him, or complimentary. Wives remember that in your marriage **God** has placed you as the **perfect companion** for your husband, a strong and fierce partner in your support of him and your family, as well as faithful in your service to, and reverence for God.

1 Peter 3:1-7 In the same way, you wives must accept the authority of your husbands. Then, even if some refuse to obey the Good News, your godly lives will speak to them without any words. They will be won over by observing your pure and reverent lives. Don't be concerned about the outward beauty of fancy hairstyles, expensive jewelry, or beautiful clothes. You should clothe yourselves instead with the beauty that comes from within, the unfading beauty of a gentle and quiet spirit, which is so precious to God. This is how the holy women of old made themselves beautiful. They put their trust in God and accepted the authority of their husbands. For instance, Sarah obeyed her husband, Abraham, and called him her master. You are her daughters when you do what is right without fear of what your husbands might do. In the same way, you husbands must give honor to your wives. Treat your wife with understanding as you live together. She may be weaker than you are, but she is your equal partner in God's gift of new life. Treat her as you should so your prayers will not be hindered.

Men if you are currently being faithful in this role, thank God for the blessings that he has provided as a result of your obedience. As your marriage has benefited from your efforts, be mindful of the significance of this directive and continue to lead without hesitation or ceasing. If this is a new concept, or you have been avoiding or neglecting this responsibility, **it is time to step up and lead**. It is not too late. God knows the impact your compliance to this command will have on your relationship with him, your wife, your family, and his kingdom. As you take that first step, seeking and asking for his direction, the Holy Spirit will provide guidance and encouragement.

There are many valuable resources which can provide excellent Bible studies, topical courses on marital issues, and information on marriage conferences that will assist in your growth and development as a couple. I have listed several below that we have enjoyed and found helpful over the years. These are just a few – you can find contact information and the services they provide through most search engines. Local churches also have classes, small group meetings, and training aids available. Online and local Christian bookstores provide a wide range of materials that are helpful, as well. Please feel free to contact me with any questions or if you need help acquiring resource materials.

James 1: 5, 6 **If you need wisdom, ask our generous God, and he will give it to you**. *He will not rebuke you for asking. But when you ask him, be sure that your faith is in God alone. Do not waver, for a person with divided loyalty is as unsettled as a wave of the sea that is blown and tossed by the wind.*

- Focus on the Family Ministries
- Family Life Ministries
- Equipping the Saints Ministries / equippingthesaints.org
- Smalley Institute
- Insight for Living
- The Five Love Languages, Gary Chapman

During the early years of our marriage, Julie and I worked at a nursing home together. As we witnessed some of the elderly couples who had been married for decades and still appeared to be in love, we would comment to each other, "I want to grow old with you." God willing, that will happen - maybe it already has. 60 seems a lot older now than when I was 25! We do not know what tomorrow holds - if 2020 has reminded us of anything, it is that reality. But we do know who holds our future and what his desires are for us. As you reflect on your past and look ahead to attaining God's will for your life, let me ask you . . . Who do you truly love? What do you make time for? What do you desire above all else? How will you invest the time that you have remaining?

Remember, a **selfless** attitude that loves **unconditionally** and will **never cease**, can only be cultivated through our relationship with Christ.

Psalms 127: 1 Unless the Lord builds a house, the work of the builders is wasted.

In the song below, "Bind us Together"[4] by Bob Gillman, we see that as we are bound together in him, that cord of three strands is not easily broken.

"Bind us together, Lord, bind us together. With cords that cannot be broken. Bind us together, Lord, bind us together. Bind us together in love.

There is only one God, there is only one King.
There is only one Body, that is why we sing.

Fit for the glory of God, purchased by his precious Son.
Born with the right to be free, for Jesus the victory has won.

We are the family of God, we are the promise divine. We are God's chosen desire, we are the glorious new wine.

Bind us together, Lord, bind us together. With cords that cannot be broken. Bind us together, Lord, bind us together. Bind us together in love."

Since God chose you to be the holy people he loves, you must clothe yourselves with tenderhearted mercy, kindness, humility, gentleness, and patience. Make allowance for each other's faults, and forgive anyone who offends you. Remember, the Lord forgave you, so you must forgive others. Above all, clothe yourselves with love, which binds us all together in perfect harmony. And let the peace that comes from Christ rule in your hearts. For as members of one body you are called to live in peace. And always be thankful. Colossians 3:12-15

Training up My Children & Grandchildren in the Lord

Train up a child in the way he should go: and when he is old, he will not depart from it. Proverbs 22:6 KJV

I imagine that this is the verse most often quoted when discussing the vital role that God has entrusted to us as parents in relation to establishing the spiritual foundation for our children. We get a better sense of the full scope of our responsibility in carrying out this command as we examine some definitions of the word **Train:**

- To develop and direct the thoughts, habits, and behavior of a child by instruction, discipline, and practice. To cause to turn, move, or point in a particular way. To actively and purposefully prepare for a competition or battle.

I picture an athlete training for hours each day, sweating and cramping, exhausting their body and mind in preparation for an upcoming event or season. They study the specific details of their responsibilities, strategies, and opponent while observing a strict diet and rest regimen, enabling them to attain their fullest potential. Their coach or training partner plays a vital role in providing additional insights, monitoring their health, keeping them motivated and re-directing their efforts when they might get off track. In high school as I prepared for the upcoming football season, I lifted weights and ran regularly to get into playing shape. I also incorporated short sprints up a neighborhood hill in hopes of increasing my speed and explosiveness. Those of you who have done hills for any type of training know that it is not an enjoyable experience – but it does produce the desired results in the long run when you remain committed to it. Training is not often easy or fun, but without it you will never achieve what you have set out to accomplish.

I see a musician practicing for years honing their skills, tirelessly and repetitiously preparing for the big performance. Their teacher patiently guiding them with the wisdom and experience gained throughout a lifetime of study. I hear the drill sergeants piercing voice reverberating through the early morning darkness demanding compliance, discipline and execution, knowing the perilous situations that wait on the battlefield and the dire consequences if they are not dedicated and adequately prepared.

These examples reinforce the difficulty and extent of the training that is necessary to be successful and victorious in any competition or battle. **As parents we must embrace our directive from God to actively and purposefully focus our efforts on pointing our children to his path, helping them establish a relationship with him, teaching them his statutes and truths, disciplining when necessary, and guiding them to discover his plan for their life.** Notice there was 3 examples given of an athlete, musician, and soldier. God has formed each child individually with their personality, talents and desires all being unique. What an amazing display of God's infinite power and creativity that he has a specific and wonderful plan for each of us. He has chosen the best path for us and has provided the parents to guide us on our journey.

Let that sink in. **God appointed you to train up the children he has blessed you with.** In Ephesians 6 we are reminded as fathers to not provoke or exasperate our children but to bring them up in a nurturing manner. As you care for and encourage your children, nourishing their spiritual growth, be mindful of their distinctive characteristics and attributes given to them by God. *Jeremiah 1:5 "I knew you before I formed you in your mother's womb. Before you were born I set you apart and appointed you as my prophet to the nations."*

In Jewish culture training up your child has always been viewed as an extremely important commitment to be taken seriously, to ensure that Biblical knowledge and traditions are taught and passed on from one generation to the next. This is addressed by Moses in *Deuteronomy 6:4-9 KJV "Hear, O Israel: The LORD our God is one LORD; and thou shalt love the LORD thy God with all thine heart, and with all thy soul, and with all they might. And these words, which I command thee this day, shall be in thine heart: **and thou shalt teach them diligently unto thy children,** and shalt talk of them when thou **sittest** in thine house, and when thou **walkest** by the way, and when thou **liest down**, and when thou **risest up**. And thou shalt bind them for a sign upon thine hand, and they shall be as frontlets between thine eyes. And thou shalt write them upon the posts of thy house, and thy gates."* This passage describes the continuous and all-encompassing manner in which they were instructed to model and teach their children in his ways, impressing on them the importance and value of the lessons they were learning.

Understand that as a parent, **you** are the person responsible for **actively** and **purposefully** imprinting God's truths upon your child and guiding them onto their path. Not their Sunday school teacher or youth group pastor. Not the staff at their Christian academy, FCA sponsor, or person who leads a Bible study. Not a relative who might have more knowledge or training than you. Those people are important and will play necessary roles in reinforcing these principles, but God has commanded you to lead in this training process, remaining steadfast and following the example set by Christ. I can guarantee that if you do not faithfully and consistently share your beliefs and values with your child using your experience to teach them, someone else will – and what they teach might be contrary to God's truths.

When our daughter Katie turned 4 we purchased our first brand new vehicle as a family. I had just turned 32 and was excited about this new experience and acquisition. Everyone remembers their first new car and every detail, the fresh paint job, the tires, the new vehicle smell. Best of all this was a convertible! Maybe not the most practical choice with three young children, but it served its purpose, with its hot pink paint job. Ok, so maybe it was a Barbie car for her birthday, but I was just happy to finally say I had bought a new car with cash.

There is an actual point to this recollection. On one of her first few road trips, her younger brother Sam was along for the ride and sitting next to her. Being a bit inexperienced behind the wheel, one of Katie's turns was a little too sharp and Sam tumbled out onto the driveway. I guess those hard plastic doors and clip latches were not designed to keep two year old boys inside of the vehicle. Now she claimed that she did not know that would happen and that she had not done it intentionally, and we believed her. But to this day, I know there still remains some doubt by Sam as to her intentions. Fortunately, since the top speed that those cars could reach was about 3 mph, EMS was not called, very little if any first aid was needed, and we have not noticed any cerebral repercussions in Sam over the years. I'm not certain, but I don't think he ever rode with her again, and yet a few years later he was thrilled to drive it after it was passed on to him and transformed into the bat mobile, thanks to Julie's painting and artistic talents.

A few years later, Katie's driving improved greatly as a result of instruction that she had received, experience that was gained, and a better awareness of her surroundings. I had failed her and Sam initially, by not providing proper direction and guidance, by not walking alongside to share insights and my knowledge, and by not keeping them from harmful situations. Teaching life skills to your children like driving a car safely are necessary and will be beneficial. However, the most important thing we must teach them as we walk alongside them, is God's Word and his plan for their life, so that they will not take a sharp turn off of the path that he has designed for them. **What good is our wisdom, and better yet God's wisdom, if it isn't shared?!**

In our society today some have the opinion that a child should choose their own path, decide who they are, what they want to believe, which direction they should pursue and how to pursue it. Many parents do not want to push their views or offer any spiritual input, believing it is best to allow their children to figure out what they prefer on their own, exploring many options along the way. Let me be clear, this mentality is the direct opposite of what God commands us to do. Children are inclined to follow the path that leads to foolishness and destruction and it requires discipline and guidance to help them avoid those paths.

- *Proverbs 13:20 KJV He that walketh with wise men shall be wise: but a companion of fools shall be destroyed.*
- *Proverbs 14:12 KJV There is a way which seemeth right unto a man, but the end thereof are the ways of death.*
- *Psalms 32:8 KJV "I will instruct thee and teach thee in the way which thou shalt go: I will guide thee with mine eye."*
- *Proverbs 16:9 KJV A man's heart deviseth his way: but the LORD directeth his steps.*

Ultimately each child will be responsible for the decisions and actions that they choose, possibly venturing down a different path than the one you have started them on. However, by providing them with continuous instruction, Biblical lessons, discipline, and a Godly example to follow, they are being prepared for the challenges they will face and might be less likely to deviate from the direction that you have helped them to establish.

Hebrews 12:5-11 And have you forgotten the encouraging words God spoke to you as his children? He said, "My child, don't make light of the Lord's discipline, and don't give up when he corrects you. For the Lord disciplines those he loves, and he punishes each one he accepts as his child. As you endure this divine discipline, remember that God is treating you as his own children. Who ever heard of a child who is never disciplined by its father? If God doesn't discipline you as he does all of his children, it means that you are illegitimate and are not really his children at all. Since we respected our earthly fathers who disciplined us, shouldn't we submit even more to the discipline of the Father of our spirits, and live forever? For our earthly fathers disciplined us for a few years, doing the best they knew how. But God's discipline is always good for us, so that we might share in his holiness. No discipline is enjoyable while it is happening - it's painful! But afterward there will be a peaceful harvest of right living for those who are trained in this way.

A favorite activity at our camp is an evening orienteering course in the woods after dark. Working in small groups with the aid of a compass and flashlight, the search for markers displaying the correct coordinates is a fun and challenging experience with lessons that offer similar parallels to our walk with Christ. We refer to the compass as his word and the truth that we need to obey to avoid poor choices or the consequences of getting lost. The lights illuminate the darkness and allow us to see the pitfalls and obstacles along our way, as well as can help us stay on the correct course in order to accomplish our goal and reach the finish (and smores!). The other group members remind us of the importance of encouragement, support, seeking wise counsel, and not having to face challenging situations on our own.

I have walked those courses hundreds of times and have had zero difficulty during the day finding the correct paths and being able to avoid the thorns and cactus. Occasionally at night, though, when I am looking for a group to monitor their progress, I get turned around and don't realize where I am, or I find myself off of the main trail, wandering through the brush and taller grass. Even with my training, years of experience, familiarity with my surroundings, and desire to move in the right direction, I can still get off course and lose the path before me.

The reality is that our children might wander off their path – by accident or intentionally – and get caught in the thorns and weeds of life. **The solid foundation that you have laid will assist in guiding them back to the straight and narrow, towards the light of Christ, the truth of his word, and away from any darkness they might encounter**. David reassures us of God's abilities and desire in *Psalms 119:105 Your word is a lamp to guide my feet and a light for my path.*

How have you approached this area of your life? Do you realize the seriousness and consequences of this command and your obedience to it? How are you spending your "free" time? What is consuming your energy and efforts? Some encouraging news is that you do not have to be seminary trained, have a child psychology degree or have the Bible memorized in order to train your children! **What you do need is to remember God's perspective, what his priorities are, and what his purpose is for you in raising your children.** Are you **actively** and **purposefully** preparing them according to God's plan?

Many parents will invest hundreds of hours and thousands of dollars over the course of their kids' childhood on various lessons, hobbies, competitions, sports, travel clubs, and other extracurricular endeavors. We did that with our children and are doing it with our grandson as well. These are beneficial, can help with their development in a variety of areas, and create family time that can be spent together – all extremely worthwhile pursuits in many ways. And yet Paul describes what our main goal should be in *I Corinthians 9:23-27 I do everything to spread the Good News and share in its blessings. Don't you realize that in a race everyone runs, but only one person gets the prize? So run to win! All athletes are disciplined in their training. They do it to win a prize that will fade away, but we do it for an eternal prize. So I run with purpose in every step. I am not just shadow boxing. I discipline my body like an athlete, training it to do what it should. Otherwise, I fear that after preaching to others I myself might be disqualified.*

Paul is talking about our motivations as a Christian and the effort and dedication required as we prepare to complete our purpose. We do not train aimlessly but instead we run the race with self-control and discipline, preparing to share the good news of the

Gospel throughout our life, unwavering in following the call of God, persevering and enduring faithfully until the end. This reward is eternal in nature and will impact us individually, as well as those whom we have served along our way.

I am not suggesting that you give up any of the activities mentioned above, just realize that you have a limited amount of meaningful, teachable time with your children and your focused effort must be wisely spent in Godly training and imprinting his truths on their lives. **Please don't sacrifice their eternal crown that will not perish, for a temporal wreath or ribbon that will**. *Proverbs 23:24 The father of godly children has cause for joy. What a pleasure to have children who are wise.*

For those of you who are grandparents, have you considered helping to train your grandchildren? What an amazing opportunity to pour into those lives, to impart to them the wisdom and experience that you have gained, and to influence that generation! *Proverbs 17:6 KJV Children's children are the crown of old men; and the glory of children are their fathers.* We have had the privilege of raising our grandson for the past 14 years and are thankful for this opportunity that God provided. God has richly blessed our family and many others through this experience. Countless numbers of lives are changed by the investments made by grandparents and other older relatives. **Don't limit God's scope of how he can use you with the time he has given you**.

Children, God has given you the command to be an active and willing participant in this process, to be obedient and teachable so that it may go well for you. *Exodus 20:12 KJV "Honour thy father and thy mother: that thy days may be long upon the land which the LORD thy God giveth thee."* He wants you to listen to instruction and correction, knowing the benefits that both will bring. **Treasure his wisdom and it will lead you to life**. *Proverbs 6:20-23 KJV My son, keep thy father's commandment, and forsake not the law of thy mother: bind them continually upon thine heart, and tie them about thy neck. When thou goest, it shall lead thee; when thou sleepest, it shall keep thee; and when thou awakest, it shall talk with thee. For the commandment is a lamp; and the law is light; and reproofs of instruction are the way of life.*

Parents, you do not have to embark on this training alone, that was never God's intention. Your church staff, Christian organizations, camps, and family members are there to assist, along with the resources available through the organizations that I listed in the previous chapter. All are well equipped with materials and insights on how to prepare and train up your child in the way they should go. His word will guide and Spirit will lead as you seek insight and wisdom.

Finally, you might be at the stage in life where your children are grown and out on their own. Maybe you wish you had spent more time training them, or been more focused on this command. Perhaps you did not realize this was your responsibility or were too busy with work and other interests. If we are honest, we all would admit that we would like a second chance occasionally. Fortunately we can still be the parent God has called us to be, he didn't give us an age limit to stop the training! You can still encourage, share insights, provide counsel, and direct conversations towards God's word and plan.

Most importantly you need to be praying for them. *James 5:16 Confess your sins to each other and pray for each other so that you may be healed. The earnest prayer of a righteous person has great power and produces wonderful results.* God knows their needs and the condition of their heart. Remember, **He created their path before they were born**. If they have lost their way or are not interested in your views or desire to assist them in their growth, do not lose hope. He has provided us with the perfect example, as he is our heavenly Father and his love is Selfless, Unconditional, and Permanent. He will continue to wait on them, never giving up, his arms open wide ready for their return. Do not doubt; just cling to the redemptive message of the prodigal son, and be ready to celebrate!

Luke 15:11-32 KJV And he said, "A certain man had two sons: and the younger of them said to his father, Father, give me the portion of goods that falleth to me. And he divided unto them his living. And not many days after the younger son gathered all together, and took his journey into a far country, and there wasted his substance with riotous living. And when he had spent all, there arose a mighty famine in that land; and he began to be in want. And he went and joined himself to a citizen of that country; and he sent him into his fields to feed swine.

And he would fain have filled his belly with the husks that the swine did eat: and no man gave unto him. And when he came to himself, he said, How many hired servants of my fathers have bread enough and to spare, and I perish with hunger! I will arise and go to my father, and will say unto him, Father, I have sinned against heaven, and before thee, and am no more worthy to be called thy son: make me as one of thy hired servants. And he arose, and came to his father. But when he was yet a great way off, his father saw him, and had compassion, and ran, and fell on his neck, and kissed him. And the son said unto him, Father, I have sinned against heaven, and in thy sight, and am no more worthy to be called thy son. But the father said to his servants, Bring forth the best robe, and put it on him; and put a ring on his hand, and shoes on his feet: and bring hither the fatted calf, and kill it; and let us eat, and be merry: for this my son was dead, and is alive again; he was lost, and is found. And they began to be merry.

Now his elder son was in the field: and as he came and drew nigh to the house, he heard musick and dancing. And he called one of the servants, and asked what these things meant. And he said unto him, Thy brother is come; and thy father hath killed the fatted calf, because he hath received him safe and sound. And he was angry, and would not go in: therefore came his father out, and intreated him. And he answering said to his father, Lo, these many years do I serve thee, neither transgressed I at any time thy commandment: and yet thou never gavest me a kid, that I might make merry with my friends: but as soon as this thy son was come, which hath devoured thy living with harlots, thou hast killed for him the fatted calf. And he said unto him, Son, thou art ever with me, and all that I have is thine. It was meet that we should make merry, and be glad: for this thy brother was dead, and is alive again; and was lost, and is found."

Our Heavenly Father is forever faithful. Unfailing and unchanging. His mercies are new every morning no matter what season we, or our children are in. His love and blessings will never cease as the lyrics in "Great is Thy Faithfulness" reassure us.

"Great is thy faithfulness, O God my Father, there is no shadow of turning with thee. Thou changest not, thy compassions, they fail not, as thou has been thou forever wilt be.

Summer and winter, and springtime and harvest, sun, moon and stars in their courses above. Join with all nature in manifold witness, to thy great faithfulness, mercy and love.

Pardon for sin and a peace that endureth, thine own dear presence to cheer and to guide. Strength for today and bright hope for tomorrow, blessings all mine, with ten thousand beside.

Great is thy faithfulness, great is thy faithfulness. Morning by morning new mercies I see. All I have needed thy hand hath provided. Great is thy faithfulness, Lord, unto me."

This hymn was first written as a poem by Thomas Chisholm about God's faithfulness over his lifetime, and referenced in the passage in *Lamentations 3:22, 23 KJV   It is of the LORD's mercies that we are not consumed, because his compassions fail not.   They are new every morning: Great is thy faithfulness.* Even nature cries out that his compassion will never fail. He provides all you will ever need - his strength for today and bright hope for tomorrow!

I have no greater joy than to hear that my children walk in the truth. 3 John 1:4 KJV

Ministering to and Actively Engaging with the Body of Christ

I want them to be encouraged and knit together by strong ties of love. I want them to have complete confidence that they understand God's mysterious plan, which is Christ himself.
Colossians 2:2, 3

Throughout the Bible we are exhorted to love and encourage one another, to pray for each other, and to not neglect meeting together in order to strengthen our relationship with God and to assist fellow believers in their growth. This continuous theme is rooted in our love for one another just as Christ loves us. Paul explains in Colossians that we are to be knit together, interlocked, and caused to unite in our faith with complete confidence in pursuit of God's plan. I like the concept of being knit or fused together, a term often used to describe how bones are healing, such as "your bones have knit together nicely." God knows the difficulties and challenges that we face and the importance of having guidance and support through all of the trials, tribulations and victories. I envision being fused – **literally joined at the hip** – with my brothers and sisters in Christ, fighting alongside one another, **battling to the end**. We have been called to action, to be purposeful and not passive, to stand together come what may, all committed to the cause of Christ and His glory. *1 Thessalonians 5:11 So encourage each other and build each other up, just as you are already doing.*

These lyrics from the classic hymn "Onward Christian Soldiers" remind us of who we are following, what lies ahead, our dependence on each other, and the final outcome of his victory. Written by Sabine Baring-Gould, his inspiration was that as Christians we are to endure hardship as good soldiers for Christ.

"Onward, Christian soldiers! Marching as to war, with the cross of Jesus going on before. Christ, the royal Master, leads against the foe; Forward into battle, see his banners go!

At the sign of triumph, Satan's host doth flee; On, then, Christian soldiers, on to victory. Hell's foundations quiver at the shout of praise; Brothers, lift your voices, loud your anthems raise.

Like a mighty army moves the Church of God; Brothers, we are treading where the Saints have trod. We are not divided; All one body we: One in hope and doctrine, one in charity.

Onward, then, ye people; Join our happy throng. Blend with ours your voices, in the triumph song: Glory, laud, and honor, Unto Christ, the King. This through countless ages, men and angels sing."

The Church of God is a mighty army and our purpose is to be united in the hope of our salvation, our growth, and charity towards one another. We follow Christ **forward** into the battle, never retreating or pausing, confident of his victory. Grasping this truth is vital to our success in living the life God has planned for us and in bringing the Gospel to the lost world around us. We must band together, drawing wisdom and inspiration from the saints who have come before us and as we are filled with the Holy Spirit's power, we will be able to drive Satan's host away.

I John 4:4-6 But you belong to God, my dear children. You have already won a victory over those people, because the Spirit who lives in you is greater than the spirit who lives in the world. Those people belong to this world, so they speak from the world's viewpoint, and the world listens to them. But we belong to God, and those who know God listen to us. If they do not belong to God, they do not listen to us. That is how we know if someone has the Spirit of truth or the spirit of deception.

Think of David, a mere teenager who was described as being "a man after God's own heart." He was filled with the Spirit, courageous, armed with 5 smooth stones, and the only one willing to stand and face a giant. But even as fearful and faithless as they had been in doubting God's ability to defeat their enemy, the Israelite army stood behind David, ready to attack the Philistines if he was somehow miraculously able to defeat their leader, Goliath. **God's intention has never been for us to fight the battles alone.** The Bible is filled with examples of God emphasizing this need of support and companionship for his followers, and performing supernatural acts throughout their lives because of their obedience and faithfulness. Noah and his family; Abraham, Sarah and Lot; Moses and Aaron; Joshua and Caleb; Rahab, her family and the spies; The Israelites marching together and collapsing the walls of Jericho; Daniel, Shadrach, Meshach, and Abednego; Esther and Mordecai; 12 disciples; Paul, Timothy, Barnabas, Silas; the Believers at Pentecost. The majority of the New Testament books were letters of instruction and encouragement written to the early churches on how to conduct themselves, grow in their faith, and the importance of staying in fellowship with one another – not going it alone.

Ephesians 5:15-20   So be careful how you live. Don't live like fools, but like those who are wise. Make the most of every opportunity in these evil days. Don't act thoughtlessly, but understand what the Lord wants you to do. Don't be drunk with wine, because that will ruin your life. Instead, be filled with the Holy Spirit, singing psalms and hymns and spiritual songs among yourselves, and making music to the Lord in your hearts. And give thanks for everything to God the Father in the name of our Lord Jesus Christ.

We worship God for who he is, what he has done for us, and what he will continue to do. When contemplating his divine nature our response is one of thanksgiving, praise and humility. *Psalms 95:1-6 KJV O come, let us sing unto the LORD: let us make a joyful noise to the rock of our salvation. Let us come before his presence with thanksgiving, and make a joyful noise unto him with psalms. For the LORD is a great God, and a great King above all gods. In his hand are the deep places of the earth: the strength of the hills is his also. The sea is his and he made it: and his hands formed the dry land. O come, let us worship and bow down: let us kneel before the LORD our Maker.*

Meeting together in the form of a corporate church setting, Sunday school or for other Biblical studies allows us to praise, worship, receive instruction, share burdens while praying for one another, and to be encouraged by others. Satan attempts to separate us from fellowship and discourages us with a convincing argument that we are going through something no one else can relate to. Remember that he is the father of lies and deceitful to his very core. The reality is that many have gone through similar situations and you need to hear their experience, advice, and reassurances. We also need to share our trials that we struggle with or that God has brought us through in order to offer hope to others. We must gather regularly to be fed, motivated, and inspired by his truths, filled with his Spirit, so that we may remain strong in our faith, be his light in a dark world, and share his hope to those who are lost.

Hebrews 11:1-6 KJV Now faith is the substance of things hoped for, the evidence of things not seen. For by it the elders obtained a good report. Through faith we understand that the worlds were framed by the word of God, so that things which are seen were not made of things which do appear. By faith Abel offered unto God a more excellent sacrifice than Cain, by which he obtained witness that he was righteous, God testifying of his gifts: and by it he being dead yet speaketh. By faith Enoch was translated that he should not see death; and was not found, because God had translated him: for before his translation he had this testimony, that he pleased God. But without faith it is impossible to please him: for he that cometh to God must believe that he is, and that he is a rewarder of them that diligently seek him.

Our faith and obedience grow stronger as we use the Spiritual gifts that he has equipped us with through our service to others, and by our participation in ministry opportunities. There are several specific gifts mentioned in 1 Corinthians chapter 12 and more are discussed throughout the New Testament. Some people have a tendency to compare their gifts, viewing someone else's talents and abilities as more important or beneficial than their own. Others can develop a prideful attitude, perceiving their talents are superior or carry a higher value. 1 Corinthians 12:11 tells me that these gifts are inspired by the Holy Spirit and were chosen specifically for me, just as he determined. Verse 18 also tells me that in fact **God has placed the parts of the body, every one of them, just as he wanted them to be!** This was not some random assignment or a cosmic crap shoot. They were chosen specifically and intentionally for me. Knowing this, I receive them with a grateful heart and use them confidently to strengthen the Body of Christ and the Kingdom of God. *I Corinthians 12:4-7 There are different kinds of spiritual gifts, but the same Spirit is the source of them all. There are different kinds of service, but we serve the same Lord. God works in different ways, but it is the same God who does the work in all of us. **A spiritual gift is given to each of us so we can help each other.***

Paul continues by identifying these following gifts: wisdom, knowledge, faith, miraculous powers, prophecy, discernment, speaking in different languages, interpretation of different languages, apostles, teaching, healing, helping and guidance. He concludes with a final appeal for empathy and unity in verses 26 and 27. *If one part suffers, all the parts suffer with it, and if one part is honored, all the parts are glad. All of you together are Christ's body, and each of you is a part of it.*

In order to plug your gifts into his service you first need to identify what they are if you have not already done that. There are many resources to assist you in discovering your individual gifts. I have used giftstest.com and found it to provide a thorough assessment, as well as several descriptions and cross references as to what the various gifts entail. You have received these from the Holy Spirit and he will guide you in identifying them, developing them, and putting them to use for God's glory.

In regards to maintaining our relationships in a manner pleasing to God, he calls on us to forgive as he has forgiven us, to be compassionate, loving others as we love ourselves. Paul explains the importance of this command in *Ephesians 4:31, 32 KJV Let all bitterness, and wrath, and anger, and clamour, and evil speaking, be put away from you, with all malice: and be ye kind one to another, tenderhearted, forgiving one another, even as God for Christ's sake hath forgiven you.* We cannot love God the way he intends for us to when we are withholding our love for others, hanging on to bitterness, anger, or resentments. As we remember what Christ has done for us, we realize that any broken relationship can and must be healed. *Proverbs 17:9 Love prospers when a fault is forgiven, but dwelling on it separates close friends.*

When our son Daniel was around 4 years old, he discovered the song by Rich Mullins, "Our God is an Awesome God."[5] He loved that song and he sang it over and over and over and . . . . you get the picture. In the house. In the Car. Before bed. As soon as he woke up. While he was playing outside. He listened to it for hours, learning every word, inflection, and point of emphasis. I dare say he could sing it as well as Rich did. An awesome song for sure, about our awesome God, so we did not mind the repetition and were touched by his passion as he would belt out the chorus.

We heard that Rich was going to be in the San Antonio area for a concert at a church so we decided to go, knowing that it would thrill Daniel. Before the concert began I needed to make a quick pit stop and as I was standing there a guy walked over and occupied the area next to me. Out of the corner of my eye I noticed that he looked a bit disheveled, not necessarily dressed for a church type concert, with long hair and a big beard. Now I have tried to not be one to judge someone by their appearance and yet I distinctly remember thinking to myself, "This guy looks a bit like a hippie, what is he doing here?"

As I rejoined Julie and Daniel and settled into my seat, I was a bit shocked as the performance got under way, and that disheveled hippie just happened to walk out onto the stage in the form of Rich Mullins. Immediately I was convicted about my judgmental assumptions, remembering that God looks at our heart and not our outward stature or appearance. *1 Samuel 16:7 But the Lord said to Samuel, "Don't judge by his appearance or height, for I have rejected him. The Lord doesn't see things the way you see them. People judge by outward appearance, but the Lord looks at the heart."*

After an amazing concert, we waited around a bit as people filed out in hopes that Daniel could meet Rich. When most of the crowd had left, we were able to talk with him and a few of his group members at the back of the church, explaining how much Daniel loved his song, and asked if he could sing a little of it for him. He was very gracious, got down on a knee so he was eye to eye, and listened intently. After the chorus, as it appeared Rich was surprised at how nicely he had sung, he began to tell him how well he had done, but Daniel was just getting started and belted out both verses and the chorus again, performing the entire rendition. Rich did not get up or try to end the song. He did not appear bored or in a hurry to be done with this encounter. He simply remained on one knee, smiling and listening patiently to a little boy who was singing his heart out about how awesome our God is. I thought to myself how wrong I was in my assumption and judgment of this man just a few hours before, based solely on his appearance. This same man on one knee listening intently to a child, I now saw as the personification of Jesus, who openly welcomed the children to gather at his feet.

Matthew 7:1-5 "Do not judge others, and you will not be judged. For you will be treated as you treat others. The standard you use in judging is the standard by which you will be judged. And why worry about a speck in your friend's eye when you have a log in your own? How can you think of saying to your friend, 'Let me help you get rid of that speck in your eye,' when you can't see past the log in your own eye? Hypocrite! First get rid of the log in your own eye; then you will see well enough to deal with the speck in your friend's eye."

What a gifted writer and performer Rich was, who God has used mightily to share his love and message. What a blessing it was to meet him and to see his love for Christ.

> "When He rolls up His sleeves He ain't just puttin on the ritz. Our God is an awesome God. There's thunder in His footsteps and lightning in His fists. Our God is an awesome God. And the Lord wasn't joking when He kicked 'em out of Eden. It wasn't for no reason that He shed His blood. His return is very close and so you better be believing that our God is an awesome God.
>
> And when the sky was starless in the void of the night. Our God is an awesome God. He spoke into the darkness and created the light. Our God is an awesome God. Judgment and wrath He poured out on Sodom, mercy and grace He gave us at the cross. I hope that we have not too quickly forgotten that our God is an awesome God.
>
> Our God is an awesome God, he reigns from heaven above. With wisdom, power, and love. Our God is an awesome God."

So let's pause and evaluate as we bring this chapter to a close. Are you actively and purposefully engaged on a regular basis with fellow believers, growing together? Strengthening one another? Spurring each other on to love and good deeds? Are you going it alone too often, fighting the war without using all of the resources that God has made available to you? Is your battle plan complete or is it lacking key strategies for success?

Are you using the gifts and talents that you have received from the Holy Spirit to strengthen your faith, assist others in their growth, minister to the needs around you, and to bring those who are lost to a saving knowledge of Jesus?

Is there someone you need to forgive and be reconciled with – anyone whom you should ask for their forgiveness so that your relationship may be restored? Any family or friends that you have been separated from over an unforgiven fault or misunderstanding? Any plank that needs to be removed or attitude that needs to be adjusted about someone else's speck?

Glory, Laud, and Honor, unto Christ the King. This through countless ages, men and angels sing. **Be joined together**. Blend your voices with other believers in that triumphant song for the ages, encouraging one another, engaged as one in the battle, continually praising our Creator, Savior, and Lord.

And they continued steadfastly in the apostles' doctrine and fellowship, and in breaking of bread, and in prayers. And fear came upon every soul: and many wonders and signs were done by the apostles. And all that believed were together, and had all things common, and sold their possessions and goods, and parted them to all men, as every man had need. And they, continuing daily with one accord in the temple, and breaking bread from house to house, did eat their meat with gladness and singleness of heart, praising God, and having favour with all the people. And the Lord added to the church daily such as should be saved. Acts 2:42-47 KJV

My Call to Evangelism and Discipleship

Jesus came and told his disciples, "I have been given all authority in heaven and on earth. Therefore, go and make disciples of all the nations, baptizing them in the name of the Father and the Son and the Holy Spirit. Teach these new disciples to obey all the commands I have given you. And be sure of this: I am with you always, even to the end of the age." Matthew 28:18-20

This passage above is known as The Great Commission in which Jesus delivers his final instructions to his disciples before his ascension to heaven, a directive intended as well for all believers throughout the ages to come. **He commands this on the basis of his authority, given to him by God the Father, which extends even beyond the boundaries of this earth and into the heavens.** David praises this authority in *Psalms 19: 1- 4 The heavens proclaim the glory of God. The skies display his craftsmanship. Day after day they continue to speak; night after night they make him known. They speak without a sound or word; their voice is never heard. Yet their message has gone throughout the earth, and their words to all the world.* Based on who God is and his plan for mankind, his exhortation in Matthew is for us to continue his mission once he has departed. To share the message of salvation, and to teach and train up disciples so they will become mature in their faith. He closes with the reassurance that he is with us always, we will never be alone.

God's desire is that all would come to know him, to put their faith and trust in him, to follow his specific and wonderful plan for them, that none should perish. We are told in Romans that his creation itself displays his power and majesty and his divine nature is clearly on display for anyone to see. He also reminds us of the consequences of foolishly trusting in our own wisdom. *Romans 1:18-23 KJV For the wrath of God is revealed from heaven against all ungodliness and unrighteousness of men, who hold the truth in unrighteousness; because that which may be known of God is manifest in them; for God hath shewed it unto them. For the invisible things of him from the creation of the world are clearly seen, being understood by the things that are made, even his eternal power and Godhead; so that they are without excuse: because that, when they knew God, they glorified him not as God, neither were thankful; but became vain in their imaginations, and their foolish* heart was darkened. *Professing themselves to be wise, they became fools, and changed the glory of the uncorruptible God into an image made like to corruptible man, and to birds, and four footed beasts, and creeping things.*

Jesus tells us that if there was no one to share his message or praise his name that the stones would cry out! *Luke 19:37-40 When he reached the place where the road started down the Mount of Olives, all of his followers began to shout and sing as they walked along, praising God for all the wonderful miracles they had seen. "Blessings on the King who comes in the name of the Lord! Peace in heaven, and glory in the highest heaven!" But some of the Pharisees among the crowd said, "Teacher, rebuke your followers for saying things like that!" He replied, "If they kept quiet, the stones along the road would burst into cheers!"*

I highlight these passages to remind us that God is omniscient, omnipotent, and omnipresent. His presence and love is apparent in all that we see, feel, and know, and his message is on display for everyone, available and waiting for their response. I realize that many Christians are hesitant about sharing their faith, concerned that they might come across as judgmental or offend someone who believes differently, or not wanting to be labeled as intolerant. Some are not confident in their knowledge of the Bible or are afraid they will not know what to say. Jesus knows our insecurities and Satan delights in creating doubt, thus limiting our obedience and rendering our witness fruitless. But Jesus also knows that when we obey, our own faith will be strengthened as we witness his life changing power at work. *Romans 1:16, 17 KJV For I am not ashamed of the gospel of Christ: for it is the power of God unto salvation to everyone that believeth; to the Jew first, and also to the Greek. For therein is the righteousness of God revealed from faith to faith: as it is written, The just shall live by faith.* He knows the blessings we will receive when sharing his good news and the joy we will experience by participating in his plan of salvation, helping to cultivate growth and maturity, as we encourage and disciple others.

You need to remember that you are sharing the most wonderful and important news anyone can hear.

Better than a "yes" to a proposal of marriage. The birth of a child. A healthy prognosis from your doctor. A promotion at work. Even better than the Publishers Clearing House showing up at your door! It is not only life-changing on this earth, but seals a home in heaven for their eternity. Whether or not someone is receptive to this message is not up to you. A lack of training, knowledge, or eloquence should not deter you or be used as an excuse to avoid this command. It is not a problem if you get tongue-tied. Remember, the Holy Spirit is in control and will lead you. Each situation is different. God just calls on us to be obedient. To be ready to give an account when prompted.

I Peter 3:15, 16 KJV But sanctify the Lord God in your hearts: and be ready always to give an answer to every man that asketh you a reason of the hope that is in you with meekness and fear: having a good conscience; that, whereas they speak evil of you, as of evildoers, they may be ashamed that falsely accuse your good conversation in Christ. Reaching out with love and concern, sharing your personal experience of what God has done in your life, that is the testimony that he desires and will bless.

God does stress our need for continued growth in our knowledge of him and that includes understanding our salvation, learning scriptures so that we can explain his plan, and familiarizing ourselves with resources that will help us be more confident when we encounter witnessing possibilities. As you pray for wisdom, opportunities to share your faith, and obedience to do so, he will provide the courage needed and the guidance you require.

Colossians 1:9-14 KJV For this cause we also, since the day we heard it, do not cease to pray for you, and to desire that ye might be filled with the knowledge of his will in all wisdom and spiritual understanding; that ye might walk worthy of the Lord unto all pleasing, being fruitful in every good work, and increasing in the knowledge of God; strengthened with all might, according to his glorious power, unto all patience and longsuffering with joyfulness; giving thanks unto the Father, which hath made us meet to be partakers of the inheritance of the saints in light: who hath delivered us from the power of darkness, and hath translated us into the kingdom of his dear Son: in whom we have redemption through his blood, even the forgiveness of sins.

We often refer to a person as being "lost" when they do not know Jesus, a statement used regularly in our lingo, and yet I do not think we fully grasp the concept of what that entails. That last verse mentions that Jesus rescued us from "the dominion of darkness," and the supreme authority over that kingdom is Satan who does not want anyone to be saved. He makes every effort to keep people in the dark spiritually, convincing them to fill any void they might sense with worldly pleasures and pursuits that will only bring temporary satisfaction. They are lovers of self yet filled with despair, drifting without direction or hope. The worldly perspective, focused inward and centered on self-reliance, is contrary to God's design. **Deep in our souls we are all searching for the meaning and purpose of our existence, and even as Satan relentlessly tries to convince us that we are not lost or in need, God has revealed his glory for all to see**. Remember Psalms 19 tells us *The heavens proclaim the glory of God. The skies display his craftsmanship. Day after day they continue to speak; night after night they make him known. They speak without a sound or word; their voice is never heard. Yet their message has gone throughout the earth, and their words to all the world.*

I have had several opportunities to explore a variety of caves over the years and have always been thankful for a dependable flashlight and an experienced guide to lead my first trips! One of the larger caves in Arkansas had several passageways with a variety of rooms on different levels that made it challenging to find your way back to the entrance until you became familiar with its layout. It was common to get turned around and to think you were going in the right direction, only to discover that you had missed a turn or had gone too far and had hit a dead end. Attempting to find your way out of any of these caves without a light would have been dangerous and led to wandering aimlessly, resulting in limited success, if any.

Growing up, I attended a church camp in northern Minnesota that was deep in the woods in a remote location that got very dark at night. I had attended that camp for many years and had walked the path from the main buildings to the cabins where we slept, hundreds of times. One evening as I was heading to the bathroom in the middle of the night, it was so dark that I could not see the path down at my feet and I became very disoriented, even though there was only one path and I knew it well. I found myself hesitating, moving slowly, worried about the trees on each side, and stopping occasionally just to get my bearings and reassure myself that I was not losing my mind.

Years ago our family was visiting friends and all of the kids were sleeping in the same room. Our youngest son Sam, who was around four at the time, was sleeping on the floor next to a bunk bed. In the middle of the night I heard him calling out for me, panic in his little voice, "Dad Help! I think I lost myself." He had rolled over underneath the bottom bunk and as the blankets were hanging down to the floor, he woke up surrounded by complete darkness, and had no idea of where he was.

These three examples point out that even in familiar surroundings we can become easily disoriented when there is a lack of light. Darkness will cause us to doubt, hesitate, and not move forward until light is shed on a situation for guidance and comfort. When you are stuck in spiritual darkness, you really are lost and will not be able to find the way out on your own.

God's plan and desires are foreign to the lost as they are disoriented and will continue to stumble along, not even realizing they are headed in the wrong direction. *Proverbs 4:19 But the way of the wicked is like total darkness. They have no idea what they are stumbling over.* That's why he calls us to be his light, to provide his truth to them as we model Christ so that we may guide them to see he is the answer they have been longing for. This is referred to as **Friendship Evangelism**, simply living our lives in a way that people can see that our hope and contentment does not originate from this world, and gives us the opportunity to share with them who our confidence and joy comes from. In the book of Matthew, Jesus commands us to love even our enemies and pray for those who persecute us. I believe that starts with asking God for their salvation. The example of Paul's conversion, literally having the light of Jesus revealed to him on the road to Damascus, encourages us that if God can take one of his greatest enemies and transform him into one of his greatest disciples, there is that same opportunity for anyone!

Matthew 5:44-48 KJV "But I say unto you, Love your enemies, bless them that curse you, do good to them that hate you, and pray for them which despitefully use you, and persecute you; that ye may be the children of your Father which is in heaven:

for he maketh his sun to rise on the evil and on the good, and sendeth rain on the just and on the unjust. For if ye love them which love you, what reward have ye? Do not even the publicans the same? And if ye salute your brethren only, what do ye more than others? Do not even the publicans so? Be ye therefore perfect, even as your Father which is in heaven is perfect." The best way we can demonstrate our love for others is by showing them God's love.

An excellent training tool that will assist in preparing you to give an account to all who ask the reason for your hope is a course entitled **Evangelism Explosion**. This will help you put your own experience into words and teach you some basic verses on salvation, enabling you to share your faith more confidently. A quote by Dietrich Bonhoeffer sums up our accountability on how we should live as a follower of Christ. **"Your life as a Christian should make nonbelievers question their disbelief in God."**[6]

Does your life reflect your profession of faith to those around you? Are your conversations and actions drawing others to Christ, causing them to inquire as to the source of your joy and peace, creating opportunities to witness? We have lost several friends in the past year, a reminder that there is no guarantee of our tomorrow. Let me encourage you to be praying for those you know who are not saved, that God would provide an opportunity for you and others to share his message with them, and that the Holy Spirit would prepare their hearts to receive it. *Matthew 9:37, 38 He said to his disciples, "The harvest is great, but the workers are few. So pray to the Lord who is in charge of the harvest; ask him to send more workers into his fields."*

Receiving guidance for a new believer is crucial in helping them as they begin to grow, and will remain vital as they continue to develop their faith in Christ. Learning about his plan for their life and understanding what is involved in the maturing process requires someone to walk alongside them, encouraging and teaching them God's truths. *John 8:31, 32 KJV Then said Jesus to those Jews which believed on him, "If ye continue in my word, then are ye my disciples indeed; and ye shall know the truth, and the truth shall make you free."*

For a plant to successfully grow it needs nutrition, water, air, space, the proper lighting and temperature, and time. When it receives all of these it will become vibrant and flourish, fulfilling its purpose. Grown in His creation, God supplies all of these needs as witnessed by beautiful fall scenery, crops at harvest time, vegetation along riverbanks, or a lush green lawn. A house plant on the other hand, depends on someone to provide for its needs or it will not survive. It always amazes me to see the initial seed or bud that grows into delicious food or a beautiful flower. Julie and I unfortunately do not have a green thumb between the two of us so witnessing that does not occur at our house very often, but when it does it is even more special!

Just as with that seed or bud, when you become a Christian you are a new creation, called to put aside – put to death – your past sinful nature and the ways of the world that you once followed, and are called to pursue Godly knowledge and his plan as your new way of life. *2 Corinthians 5:17, 18 KJV Therefore if any man be in Christ, he is a new creature: old things are passed away; behold, all things are become new. And all things are of God, who hath reconciled us to himself by Jesus Christ, and hath given to us the ministry of reconciliation.* God's command is for the more mature Christians to train and nurture new believers with our spiritual "green thumb," to share our lives, experience, and wisdom as essential ingredients to their growth. As we fellowship, spend time in prayer and study his word together, we are reminded by Timothy that God's truth has the power to change all lives. *2 Timothy 3:16, 17 KJV All scripture is given by inspiration of God, and is profitable for doctrine, for reproof, for correction, for instruction in righteousness: that the man of God may be perfect, throughly furnished unto all good works.*

We had the opportunity a few years ago to visit the Redwoods and stood in awe at their size as well as their age. Towering hundreds of feet above us, amazed as we thought of all the years they had been there, we remembered that those majestic trees had started out as a tiny seed so long ago. **Like any plant or tree, guiding someone's spiritual transformation will take time – yet your investment in that life, helping them to develop the attitude and attributes of Christ, will reap eternal rewards!**

Jesus calls us to follow his example of selfless love, humility, and concern for others interests over our own, and to testify of God's glory. *Philippians 2:1-11 Is there any encouragement from belonging to Christ? Any comfort from his love? Any fellowship together in the Spirit? Are your hearts tender and compassionate? Then make me truly happy by agreeing wholeheartedly with each other, loving one another, and working together with one mind and purpose. Don't be selfish; don't try to impress others. Be humble, thinking of others as better than yourselves. Don't look out for your own interests, but take an interest in others, too. You must have the attitude that Christ Jesus had. Though he was God, he did not think of equality with God as something to cling to. Instead, he gave up his divine privileges; he took the humble position of a slave and was born as a human being. When he appeared in human form, he humbled himself in obedience to God and died a criminal's death on a cross. Therefore, God elevated him to the place of highest honor and gave him the name above all other names, that at the name of Jesus every knee should bow, in heaven and on earth and under the earth, and every tongue declare that Jesus Christ is Lord, to the glory of God the Father.*

We must view this training as a lifelong pursuit and responsibility. You will not reach a certain age or maturity level where you have done enough, are too old, or are out of touch. **There is no retirement from discipling others!** Continue to train up those God brings across your path, preparing them as they learn from your instruction and example, so that they will invest the same discipleship principles with others. *Titus 2:1-8 KJV But speak thou the things which become sound doctrine: that the aged men be sober, grave, temperate, sound in faith, in charity, in patience. The aged women likewise, that they be in behaviour as becometh holiness, not false accusers, not given to much wine, teachers of good things; that they may teach the young women to be sober, to love their husbands, to love their children, to be discreet, chaste, keepers at home, good, obedient to their own husbands, that the word of God be not blasphemed. Young men likewise exhort to be sober minded. In all things shewing thyself a pattern of good works: in doctrine shewing uncorruptness, gravity, sincerity, sound speech, that cannot be condemned; that he that is of the contrary part may be ashamed, having no evil thing to say of you.*

This passage is another great encouragement for us to continue to train and pray for our children and future generations that they would seek his wisdom, be filled with patience and love, walking in integrity and truth, always growing in their knowledge of God.

God has given each of us the responsibility to disciple others – we must share his truths. There is someone whom he has in mind for you to guide and help realize who they are in Christ and the power he yields for their life. As you seek to be obedient in this area, he will provide all of the wisdom and insights that you will need as well as the person to shepherd, accomplishing the good work he has ordained for you to do.

Ephesians 4:11-16 KJV And he gave some, apostles; and some, prophets, and some evangelists; and some pastors and teachers; for the perfecting of the saints, for the work of the ministry, for the edifying of the body of Christ: till we all come in the unity of the faith, and of the knowledge of the Son of God, unto a perfect man, unto the measure of the stature of the fullness of Christ: that we henceforth be no more children, tossed to and fro, and carried about with every wind of doctrine, by the sleight of men, and cunning craftiness, whereby they lie in wait to deceive; but speaking the truth in love, may grow up into him in all things, which is the head, even Christ: from whom the whole body fitly joined together and compacted by that which every joint supplieth, according to the effectual working in the measure of every part, maketh increase of the body unto the edifying of itself in love.

My favorite song at our church camp when I was growing up was the classic, "Pass it on"[7] by Kurt Kaiser. Gathered around the campfire as eleven and twelve year olds, our favorite part was obviously shouting from the mountain top "PRAISE GOD" as loudly as we could, while as we grew older we appreciated the message of his love and were challenged to pass his message on.

> "It only takes a spark to get a fire going. And soon all those around can warm up in its glowing; That's how it is with God's love, once you've experienced it. You spread his love, to everyone, you want to pass it on.

What a wondrous time is spring, when all the trees are budding. The birds begin to sing, the flowers start their blooming; That's how it is with God's love, once you've experienced it. You want to sing, it's fresh like spring, you want to pass it on.

I wish for you my friend this happiness that I've found. You can depend on Him, it matters not where you're bound. I'll shout it from the mountain top, Praise God! I want the world to know. The Lord of love has come to me, I want to pass it on."

So we tell others about Christ, warning everyone and teaching everyone with all the wisdom God has given us. We want to present them to God, perfect in their relationship to Christ. That's why I work and struggle so hard, depending on Christ's mighty power that works within me. Colossians 1:28, 29

Laboring for God's Glory

Work willingly at whatever you do, as though you were working for the Lord rather than for people. Remember that the Lord will give you an inheritance as your reward, and that the master you are serving is Christ. Colossians 3:23, 24

The majority of us will spend a good portion of our life investing significant time and effort into our occupations. Often we refer to the people who we work with as our second family, developing close bonds and spending more time each day with our co-workers than with our actual family members. Your calling at this time could be working at home, managing the household duties, daily chores, running errands and fixing meals. The laundry basket is never empty, toys and clothes strewn about, on the go from one lesson to the next practice. You might be past this stage, settled into retirement, busy writing the next chapter of your story. Your days spent pursuing recreational interests, hobbies you have put off that you now have found time for, reconnecting with family, or engaging in volunteer opportunities.

The above passage instructs us to remember that in whatever we are doing and whichever season of life we are currently in, we should concentrate all of our energy and focus on pleasing and glorifying God, using the talents that he has given us to serve the Lord.

We have a natural tendency to assume that our abilities and opportunities come from within us, a result of our training, sacrifice, and hard work, so we look proudly on our accomplishments and take credit for any success. Jeremiah reminds us that the "self- made man" line is not the way it works and that everything is from the Lord and to be used for his glory. *Jeremiah 9:23, 24 KJV Thus saith the LORD, "Let not the wise man glory in his wisdom, neither let the mighty man glory in his might, let not the rich man glory in his riches: but let him that glorieth glory in this, that he understandeth and knoweth me, that I am the LORD which exercise lovingkindness, judgment, and righteousness, in the earth: for in these things I delight, saith the LORD."* He has blessed you with your talents, the desire and provisions necessary to develop them, the education and training you have received, and every opportunity that you have been given. Acknowledging this creates a humble and grateful heart for his unfailing love, an appreciation for his fairness and justice, and the ability to focus all of your praise on his glory and righteousness.

As we learn to view everything from his perspective our priorities then line up accordingly, allowing us to accomplish our purpose, which he has already planned for us. These Proverbs remind us of his role in "our success."

- *Proverbs 16:3 KJV Commit thy works unto the LORD, and thy thoughts shall be established.*
- *Proverbs 19:21 You can make many plans, but the Lord's purpose will prevail.*

We are warned by Jesus that we cannot serve two masters, as loyalty to one leads to temporal satisfaction while the other guides us to eternal rewards. It is our decision which course to pursue, which one we will seek, and which one will satisfy our needs.

Matthew 6:24-33 KJV "No man can serve two masters: for either he will hate the one, and love the other; or else he will hold to the one, and despise the other. Ye cannot serve God and mammon. Therefore I say unto you, take no thought for your life, what ye shall eat, or what ye shall drink; nor yet for your body, what ye shall put on. Is not the life more than meat, and the body than raiment? Behold the fowls of the air: for they sow not, neither do they reap, nor gather into barns; yet your heavenly Father feedeth them. Are ye not much better than they? Which of you by taking thought can add one cubit unto his stature? And why take ye thought for raiment? Consider the lilies of the field, how they grow; they toil not, neither do they spin: and yet I say unto you, that even Solomon in all his glory was not arrayed like one of these. Wherefore, if God so clothe the grass of the field, which today is, and tomorrow is cast into the oven, shall he not much more clothe you, O ye of little faith? Therefore take no thought, saying, What shall we eat? or, What shall we drink? or, Wherewithal shall we be clothed? (For after all these things do the Gentiles seek:) for your heavenly Father knoweth that ye have need of all these things. But seek ye first the kingdom of God, and his righteousness; and all these things shall be added unto you." When reading about the lilies' splendor, I always picture the Texas hill country bluebonnets, the vast array of colors covering the hillsides in the spring, providing spectacular views for a few weeks until they suddenly are no more. As you seek his kingdom above all else, live as he calls you to live and use your talents for his glory, he will provide all that you need.

Once we truly embrace the reality that everything we have is from God and that he delights when we share the blessings he bestowed upon us with others, we will desire to give more to those in need from our abundance that he has so graciously provided. In Paul's letter to the Hebrews he points out what pleases God. *Hebrews 6:10-12   For God is not unjust. He will not forget how hard you have worked for him and how you have shown your love to him by caring for other believers, as you still do. Our great desire is that you will keep on loving others as long as life lasts, in order to make certain that what you hope for will come true. Then you will not become spiritually dull and indifferent. Instead, you will follow the example of those who are going to inherit God's promises because of their faith and endurance.*

Along with our financial resources we must also look for opportunities to willingly share our time, expertise, experience, and love with those we work with and interact with each day. *Hebrews 13:16   And don't forget to do good and to share with those in need. These are the sacrifices that please God.*   As you reach out in kindness showing your concern and helping to meet a need, you will also be sharing God's love and pointing them towards his plan for their life. In the book of Matthew, Jesus uses the two most familiar metaphors of how our actions should have an impact on the world, serving as salt and light. *Matthew 5:13-16 "You are the salt of the earth. But what good is salt if it has lost its flavor? Can you make it salty again? It will be thrown out and trampled underfoot as worthless. You are the light of the world – like a city on a hilltop that cannot be hidden. No one lights a lamp and then puts it under a basket. Instead, a lamp is placed on a stand, where it gives light to everyone in the house. In the same way, let your good deeds shine out for all to see, so that everyone will praise your heavenly Father."*

We are called to let our good deeds shine forth, to confidently proclaim God's mercy and grace for all to see. It has always amazed me how on a dark night a small light can illuminate a large area, allowing us to see clearly and to move without hesitation. If you have ever been too close when headlights have been turned on it can have a blinding effect. Very powerful. Hundreds of feet are suddenly visible that were pitch black just a moment before. **Jesus longs for our actions to point to God so intensely that his radiant message cannot be ignored or dismissed.** Salt was used mainly as a preservative for thousands of years and its reference here was to emphasize the importance of preserving their purity and witness to God's truths. It also refers to its ability to enhance flavor when the correct amount is applied or how it is likely to leave a bad taste if too much is added. When our speech is seasoned with love, joy, peace, patience, kindness, goodness, faithfulness, gentleness, and self-control, our message will be the most desirable to hear.

God has given us the talents and interests that we are best suited for knowing that we will receive pleasure and satisfaction as we put them to use for his glory. *Ephesians 2:10 For we are God's masterpiece. He has created us anew in Christ Jesus, so we can do the good things he planned for us long ago.* His desire is for us to enjoy the fruits of our labor as we are faithful in doing what he has already planned.

Some of you might be in the midst of a difficult struggle, sensing a lack of direction in your work, not finding fulfillment, knowing you need a change. As we rely on God during trying periods, remember that he will sustain us and use any trial to strengthen and mold us, if we allow him to. As you call out to the Lord, waiting patiently for his timing and leading, be comforted by his instruction to Joshua *1:9 "This is my command – be strong and courageous! Do not be afraid or discouraged. For the Lord your God is with you wherever you go."* We are reassured in *Psalms 46:1 KJV God is our refuge and strength, a very present help in trouble.*

Finally, we are encouraged that as we rest in the Lord he will renew our strength. His example of rest after he created the world is important for us to follow so that our health will remain strong and that we will honor him with a consistent time of worship to focus on his blessings. *Genesis 2:1-3 KJV Thus the heavens and the earth were finished, and all the host of them. And on the seventh day God ended his work which he had made; and he rested on the seventh day from all his work which he had made. And God blessed the seventh day, and sanctified it: because that in it he had rested from all his work which God created and made.* As we wait on him, we are assured of our eternal victory. *Psalms 62:1, 2 I wait quietly before God, for my victory comes from him. He alone is my rock and my salvation, my fortress where I will never be shaken.*

Dr. Martin Luther King Jr. addressed what our attitude and effort should entail, no matter what our line of work is. "If a man is called to be a street sweeper, he should sweep streets even as Michelangelo painted, or Beethoven composed music, or Shakespeare wrote poetry. He should sweep streets so well that all the hosts of heaven and earth will pause to say, here lived a great street sweeper who did his job well."[8] Whatever God's calling is for your life, he has a purpose for you. If you will allow him to, he will complete it and be glorified in the process, as he is able to accomplish so much more than we can imagine.

This passage below, followed by an eternal view into heaven of our Triune Lord God Almighty written by Reginald Heber, reminds us of who's power we possess.

Ephesians 3:14-21 KJV For this cause I bow my knees unto the Father of our Lord Jesus Christ, of whom the whole family in heaven and earth is named, that he would grant you, according to the riches of his glory, to be strengthened with might by his Spirit in the inner man; that Christ may dwell in your hearts by faith; that ye, being rooted and grounded in love, may be able to comprehend with all saints what is the breadth, and length, and depth, and height; and to know the love of Christ, which passeth knowledge, that ye might be filled with all the fulness of God. Now unto him that is able to do exceeding abundantly above all that we ask or think, according to the power that worketh in us, unto him be glory in the church by Christ Jesus throughout all ages, world without end. Amen

> "Holy, Holy, Holy! Lord God Almighty! Early in the morning our song shall rise to thee. Holy, Holy, Holy, merciful and mighty! God in three persons, blessed Trinity!

Holy, Holy, Holy! All the saints adore thee. Casting down their golden crowns around the glassy sea. Cherubim and seraphim falling down before thee. Who wert and art and evermore shall be.

Holy, Holy, Holy! Though the darkness hide thee. Though the eye of sinful man thy glory may not see. Only thou are holy, there is none beside thee. Perfect in power, in love and purity.

Holy, Holy, Holy! Lord God Almighty! All thy works shall praise thy name in earth, and sky, and sea. Holy, Holy, Holy! Merciful and mighty! God in three persons, blessed Trinity!"

Is your identity and sense of worth based on what you do for a living, or is it based *on who you are living for*? Does God receive the praise and glory from your success? Do your actions and speech reveal evidence of your relationship with Christ? Are you seeking opportunities to build God's kingdom through sharing his blessings with those in need?

Love each other with genuine affection, and take delight in honoring each other. Never be lazy, but work hard and serve the Lord enthusiastically. Rejoice in our confident hope. Be patient in trouble, and keep on praying. When God's people are in need, be ready to help them. Always be eager to practice hospitality.
Romans 12:10-13

Honoring His Temple

*Don't you realize that your body is the temple of the Holy Spirit,
who lives in you and was given to you by God? You do not
belong to yourself, for God bought you with a high price. So you
must honor God with your body. 1 Corinthians 6:19, 20*

A common phrase that is used during a conversion experience
after asking for God's forgiveness and salvation, is to "ask Jesus
to come into your life and take control." The result of this
invitation is that the Holy Spirit responds and dwells within you
so that he can provide comfort, guidance and wisdom as you
surrender the Lordship of your life. Our body is no longer our
own to do with as we please. It is now described as his temple,
home to the Spirit of the Almighty God. We bring praise and
honor to him as we protect and care for each area of this temple,
obediently pursuing a righteous and pure heart. *Proverbs 4:23
Guard your heart above all else, for it determines the course of
your life.*

Our heart is continually pumping blood to every area of our body,
focused solely on that purpose and vital to our survival. This
circulation process takes less than sixty seconds to reach every
cell and must occur nonstop for us to live. God knows that in
order for us to realize the plans and blessings he has prepared
for us we need a heart transplant – removing our old, sinful
nature – and replacing it with a new one, which is found in
Christ, and allows his truths to course through our veins. *Psalms
51:10 KJV Create in me a clean heart, O God; and renew a right
spirit within me.* **He knows that everything we pursue is
influenced by what our heart desires and will determine
the spiritual, emotional, and physical condition of our
temple.** *Jeremiah 17:10 KJV "I the LORD search the heart, I
try the reins, even to give every man according to his ways, and
according to the fruit of his doings."*

Paul reminds us that our worship of God is reflected in the way
we live our lives. Once we have had that heart transplant, our
minds can be renewed to follow his perfect will, not our own,
and not the worlds - which offers vain and temporal satisfactions.
*Romans 12:1, 2 KJV I beseech you therefore, brethren, by the
mercies of God, that ye present your bodies a living sacrifice, and
holy, acceptable unto God, which is your reasonable service. Be*

not conformed to this world: but be ye transformed by the renewing of your mind, that ye may prove what is that good, and acceptable, and perfect, will of God. As we desire to please God by setting our minds on the things above, our temple will be transformed and we will reflect his priorities, perspective, and purpose. *Colossians 3:1-4 KJV If ye then be risen with Christ, seek those things which are above, where Christ sitteth on the right hand of God. Set your affection on things above, not on things on the earth. For ye are dead, and your life is hid with Christ in God. When Christ, who is our life, shall appear, then shall ye also appear with him in glory.*

Like blood flowing through us, the renewing of our mind needs to happen continually so we must train our bodies to be used for his glory and to live for eternal rewards. *1 Timothy 4:8 KJV "For bodily exercise profiteth little: but godliness is profitable unto all things, having promise of the life that now is, and of that which is to come."*

Even though we live in the world, we have a heavenly home and are instructed not to be consumed by the cares and the things of this world. However much they entice us we must remember the death that they will lead to, and allow his Spirit to guide us to what is true, honorable, right, pure, lovely, and admirable. We must set our minds on what is above, not on this earth. **As we focus on whatever is excellent and worthy of praise, we create a dwelling place suitable for the Holy Spirit**.

Several verses address how our physical and mental health is directly related to specific actions or attitudes and how that can affect our mind or body, strengthening or causing harm to our temple.

- *Proverbs 17:22 KJV A merry heart doeth good like a medicine: but a broken spirit drieth the bones.*
- *Proverbs 16:24 KJV Pleasant words are as an honeycomb, sweet to the soul, and health to the bones.*
- *Proverbs 4:20-22 KJV My son, attend to my words; incline thine ear unto my sayings. Let them not depart from thine eyes; keep them in the midst of thine heart. For they are life unto those that find them, and health to all their flesh.*

- *Proverbs 3:7, 8 KJV Be not wise in thine own eyes: Fear the LORD, and depart from evil. It shall be health to thy navel, and marrow to thy bones.*

Often when this topic of our body being God's temple is discussed, the message is to not drink, smoke, do drugs, or over eat, and to exercise so that we take the best care possible of our physical body. There are many verses in the Bible that refer to all of these issues in some form, thus lending validity for us to obediently seek God's plan for this part of his temple.

- *1 Corinthians 10:31 KJV Whether therefore ye eat, or drink, or whatsoever ye do, do all to the glory of God.*
- *Ephesians 5:18 Don't be drunk with wine, because that will ruin your life. Instead, be filled with the Holy Spirit.*
- *Proverbs 23:19-21 My child, listen and be wise: Keep your heart on the right course. Do not carouse with drunkards or feast with gluttons, for they are on their way to poverty, and too much sleep clothes them in rags.*
- *2 Timothy 1:7 For God has not given us a spirit of fear and timidity, but of power, love, and self-discipline.*
- *Proverbs 13:4 KJV The soul of the sluggard desireth, and hath nothing: but the soul of the diligent shall be made fat.*
- *Titus 2:11-14 KJV For the grace of God that bringeth salvation hath appeared to all men, teaching us that, denying ungodliness and worldly lusts, we should live soberly, righteously, and godly, in this present world; looking for that blessed hope, and the glorious appearing of the great God and our Saviour Jesus Christ; who gave himself for us, that he might redeem us from all iniquity, and purify unto himself a peculiar people, zealous of good works.*

It's not my intent to suggest to you what you should eat or drink, or how to live your life, as there are many ways to interpret verses on these topics. Many have physical and health issues beyond their control. I would simply encourage you to look at these areas and ask God for guidance as to his desires for you. I am confident that he will reveal his perfect plan and guide you with confidence along that path. He knows that the healthier we are, the more involved in his work we can be, ready to answer his call in our service to others. Remember, the plan he has for our lives while on this earth, working for his glory and sharing his message with others, does not end until he calls us to our eternal home.

*2 Corinthians 4:13-18 But we continue to preach because we have the same kind of faith the psalmist had when he said, "I believe in God, so I spoke." We know that God, who raised the Lord Jesus, will also raise us with Jesus and present us to himself together with you. All of this is for your benefit. And as God's grace reaches more and more people, there will be great thanksgiving, and God will receive more and more glory. That is why we never give up. Though our bodies are dying, **our spirits are being renewed every day**. For our present troubles are small and won't last very long. Yet they produce for us a glory that vastly outweighs them and will last forever! So we don't look at the troubles we can see now; rather, **we fix our gaze on things that cannot be seen**. For the things we see now will soon be gone, but the things we cannot see will last forever.*

As you fix your gaze on Jesus, the cares of this world will fade away. Helen Lemmel wrote "Turn your eyes upon Jesus" after being inspired by a tract that she had received from a friend. The lyrics remind us of the importance of fixing our gaze on him and its necessity in order to stay fully engaged in the race he has called us to run, to keep our focus on his glory and grace, thankful that he sits on the throne of our temple.

"O soul, are you weary and troubled? No light in the darkness you see? There's light for a look at the Savior, and life more abundant and free.

Through death into life everlasting, He passed and we follow him there. Over us sin no more hath dominion, for more than conquerors we are.

His word shall not fail you, he promised, believe him and all will be well. Then go to a world that is dying, his perfect salvation to tell!

Turn your eyes upon Jesus. Look full in his wonderful face. And the things of earth will grow strangely dim, in the light of His glory and grace."

What an amazing and powerful reminder that as believers and followers of Christ we are honored and blessed to personally house the **King of Kings** and **Lord of Lords**!

Alpha and Omega	The Beginning and the End
Yahweh	Lord, Jehovah
Adonai	Lord, Master
El Elyon	The Most High God
Jehovah Nissi	The Lord My Banner
Jehovah Rapha	The Lord That Heals
Jehovah Shammah	The Lord Is There
Jehovah Jireh	The Lord Will Provide
Jehovah Shalom	The Lord Is Peace
Jehovah Sabaoth	The Lord Of Hosts
Jehovah Tsidkenu	The Lord Our Righteousness
Jehovah Mekoddishkem	The Lord Who Sanctifies You
Jehovah Raah	The Lord My Shepherd
El Olam	The Everlasting God
El Shaddai	Lord God Almighty

We press on with continual praise, worshiping and bringing glory to **His Name** in all that we do. He created you. He knew you before you were born and he knit you together in your mother's womb. He knows your every thought and action before you do. His watch over you is constant and his blessings are endless. **Who better to sit on the throne of your temple than your Father who is in heaven**. Hallowed be his name. His kingdom come. His will be done. On earth as it is in heaven!

Psalms 139 KJV O LORD, thou hast searched me, and known me. Thou knowest my downsitting and mine uprising, thou understandest my thought afar off. Thou compassest my path and my lying down, and art acquainted with all my ways. For there is not a word in my tongue, but, lo, O LORD, thou knowest it altogether. Thou hast beset me behind and before, and laid thine hand upon me. Such knowledge is too wonderful for me; it is high, I cannot attain unto it. Whither shall I go from thy spirit? Or whither shall I flee from thy presence? If I ascend up into heaven, thou art there: if I make my bed in hell, behold, thou are there. If I take the wings of the morning, and dwell in the uttermost parts of the sea; even there shall thy hand lead me, and thy right hand shall hold me. If I say, Surely the darkness shall cover me; even the night shall be light about me. Yea, the darkness hideth not from thee; but the night shineth as the day: the darkness and the light are both alike to thee. For thou hast possessed my reins: thou hast covered me in my mother's womb. I will praise thee; for I am fearfully and wonderfully made: Marvellous are thy works; and that my soul knoweth right well. My substance was not hid from thee, when I was made in secret, and curiously wrought in the lowest parts of the earth. Thine eyes did see my substance, yet being unperfect; and in thy book all my members were written, which in continuance were fashioned, when as yet there was none of them. How precious also are thy thoughts unto me, O God! How great is the sum of them! If I should count them, they are more in number than the sand: when I awake, I am still with thee. Surely thou wilt slay the wicked, O God: depart from me therefore, ye bloody men. For they speak against thee wickedly, and thine enemies take thy name in vain. Do not I hate them, O LORD, that hate thee? And am not I grieved with those that rise up against thee? I hate them with perfect hatred: I count them mine enemies.

Search me, O God, and know my heart: try me and know my thoughts: and see if there be any wicked way in me, and lead me in the way everlasting.

"Because He Lives"[9] written by Bill and Gloria Gaither, reaffirms the power of the Holy Spirit in our lives and the presence of his calming peace.

> "God sent his Son, they called him Jesus, he came to love, heal and forgive; He lived and died to buy my pardon, an empty grave is there to prove my Savior lives!
>
> How sweet to hold a newborn baby, and feel the pride and joy he gives; But greater still the calm assurance, this child can face uncertain days because He lives!
>
> And then one day, I'll cross the river, I'll fight life's final war with pain; And then, as death gives way to victory, I'll see the lights of glory and I'll know He lives!

Because He lives, I can face tomorrow, because He lives, all fear is gone; Because I know He holds the future, and life is worth the living, just because He lives!"

Praise God for an empty tomb! Praise God for his calm assurance during these uncertain times! Praise God for his ultimate victory over fear, sin and death! Praise God that he lives and that he holds our future!

As you examine the health of your heart are you aware of God's desires for you? Who is on the throne in your temple? What are you allowing to influence you - what do you listen to, watch, look at, think about throughout your day? Our brain is often compared to a computer, able to recall events and details throughout all stages of our life. **Do you realize the impact of what your mind is set on?** Are you resting in Christ and his word or are the cares of this world overwhelming you?

Dear brothers and sisters, pattern your lives after mine, and learn from those who follow our example. For I have told you often before, and I say it again with tears in my eyes, that there are many whose conduct shows they are really enemies of the cross of Christ. They are headed for destruction. Their god is their appetite, they brag about shameful things, and they think only about this life here on earth. But we are citizens of heaven, where the Lord Jesus Christ lives. And we are eagerly waiting for him to return as our Savior. He will take our weak mortal bodies and change them into glorious bodies like his own, using the same power with which he will bring everything under his control.
Philippians 3:17-21

Storing My Treasures in Heaven

"Don't store up treasures here on earth, where moths eat them and rust destroys them, and where thieves break in and steal. Store your treasures in heaven, where moths and rust cannot destroy, and thieves do not break in and steal. Wherever your treasure is, there the desires of your heart will also be."
Matthew 6:19-21

As we are drawn once again to examine the desires of our heart, I'm getting the sense that this is on God's top 3 list of the most important concepts that he calls us to embrace! Love God. Love others. Guard the desires of your heart. **All that we treasure originates in our heart with what we choose to desire**. Our heart is our core, located in the center of our body and described as the *well-spring* from which everything else flows, affecting every area of our life. This term is commonly referred to as the head or beginning of a natural spring, described as an original and bountiful source. It continuously nourishes and sustains all forms of life around it, as well as for many miles downstream. If it were to dry up, be diverted, or become toxic, everything that had benefited from its flow would be affected, its growth stunted, or even killed.

Your response to all of God's commands flows from whether or not you desire to obey them. To love God with all of your heart, soul, and mind. To remember that he is the only god and to not make any idols of other gods. To not take his name in vain. To keep the Sabbath day holy. To honor your father and mother. To not murder, steal, or commit adultery. To not bear false witness against your neighbor or covet anything they have. To refrain from gossip and idle chatter. To care for the widow and orphan. To honor his temple. To train up your children. To love your spouse as he loves his church. To meet with and encourage fellow believers. To share his good news to a lost world. To shepherd and disciple his flock. To do all you do for his glory. To love your neighbor as yourself. **Obedience to these commands is a result of your heart desiring what God has intended for you, which is far greater than anything you can imagine or plan for yourself.** The desires that flow from your heart direct every action, word, thought, and motive, and will lead to many blessings in this world and eternal rewards, if you choose them wisely.

1 Timothy 6:17-19 KJV Charge them that are rich in this world, that they be not high minded, nor trust in uncertain riches, but in the living God, who giveth us richly all things to enjoy; that they do good, that they be rich in good works, ready to distribute, willing to communicate; laying up in store for themselves a good foundation against the time to come, that they may lay hold on eternal life.

We are instructed in Proverbs 4:23 to guard our heart above all else as it determines the course of our life. We guard what is valuable, what is deemed important and is worth the trouble or expense because of its significance. Millions of dollars are spent protecting homes, possessions, life savings, and investments. But placing our security, hope, or trust in these is unreliable as they will be consumed, destroyed or stolen. They are all temporal and eventually will appear no more. **Our treasure that is stored in heaven however, is eternal, guarded by God, and will never perish**.

We also need to guard our heart against Satan's attacks as he knows the role it plays in all of our decision making. He deceptively convinces us that the apple is not bad for us and that God's plan will diminish our enjoyment of worldly pleasures. As he plants seeds of doubt and subtly misleads us about what we should strive to attain or what we deserve, we can become confused, resentful, and discouraged, easily swayed concerning which treasures to pursue. Satan is constantly attempting to harden your heart to the things of God, gradually moving your desires away from him and others, to a focus centered on yourself. As he dangles beautiful material trinkets along our path, tempting us to stop and consider their worth, we are in danger of allowing our love for God and his eternal treasure to be replaced for a love of stuff that will at best, bring short term, temporal enjoyment. *1 Timothy 6:9, 10 KJV But they that will be rich fall into temptation and a snare, and into many foolish and hurtful lusts, which drown men in destruction and perdition. For the love of money is the root of all evil: which while some coveted after, they have erred from the faith, and pierced themselves through with many sorrows.*

Paul warns that when our love of money and our pursuit of acquiring worldly treasures replace our love for God, our faith can be weakened, our witness is less effective, and our lives will be

unfulfilled. **If you've lost your way or have been fooled by the lies and have been running after and storing up treasures that will pass away, Jesus tells us that it's not too late to return to your first love**. *Revelation 2:1-5 KJV*
"Unto the angel of the church of Ephesus write: These things saith he that holdeth the seven stars in his right hand, who walketh in the midst of the seven golden candlesticks; I know thy works, and thy labour, and thy patience, and how thou canst not bear them which are evil: and thou hast tried them which say they are apostles, and are not, and hast found them liars: and hast borne, and hast patience, and for my name's sake hast laboured, and hast not fainted. Nevertheless I have somewhat against thee, because thou hast left thy first love. Remember therefore from whence thou art fallen, and repent, and do the first works; or else I will come unto thee quickly, and will remove thy candlestick out of his place, except thou repent."

Initially they were commended for working hard, enduring patiently, not tolerating evil, and suffering for him without quitting. But God knew the desires of their heart had changed and that the integral piece of their obedience that had led them to focus on his eternal works was askew. The issue was that their love had faded, for God and for each other. He knew Satan was infiltrating their hearts, attempting to lead them astray from what their purpose was, thus his exhortation for them to return to their first love.

As we fully comprehend that God is the giver of life, the one who offers salvation, and that he has blessed us with every gift we have received, our response to his love and generosity will result in our pursuit of heavenly treasure and bringing all glory to him. **Those are the treasures that will last for eternity - souls and the word of God**. These are the treasures that we should be seeking during our remaining time here on this earth: memorizing his word and following his instructions obediently, showing his love and mercy to those around us, sharing his message of salvation, and helping others grow to a full maturity in Christ. He has given us many gifts, opportunities and resources, all to be enjoyed but also to be used for this purpose - for people to come to know him, and for us to know and love him more. Live the life that he's already planned for you as he will never fail you, enjoying his blessings here with the time you have remaining, while storing up treasures in your eternal home.

Hebrews 13:5 KJV Let your conversation be without covetousness; and be content with such things as ye have: for he hath said, "I will never leave thee, nor forsake thee."

He has called us to be faithful stewards of all that he has entrusted to us as he knows what we are capable of. Jesus reminds us that we are accountable to use what God has provided to each of us. The emphasis here is not just on wealth, but on every aspect of what we have and who we are. Our life, health, talents, intellect, relationships, finances and time should all be held with an open hand, viewed as his possessions, not ours. He knows that as we give with a grateful heart, we will experience a satisfaction and fulfillment that is far greater than any pleasure that we would have received from that next phone upgrade, newest gaming system, matching piece of furniture, or 80 inch TV.

Jesus tells us to avoid all forms of greed and the peril that awaits those who arrogantly think that they control their own future. *Luke 12:15-21 KJV And he said unto them, "Take heed, and beware of covetousness: for a man's life consisteth not in the abundance of the things which he possesseth." And he spake a parable unto them, saying, "The ground of a certain rich man brought forth plentifully: and he thought within himself, saying, What shall I do, because I have no room where to bestow my fruits? And he said, This will I do: I will pull down my barns, and build greater; and there will I bestow all my fruits and my goods. And I will say to my soul, Soul, thou hast much goods laid up for many years; take thine ease, eat, drink, and be merry. But God said unto him, Thou fool, this night thy soul shall be required of thee: then whose shall those things be, which thou hast provided? So is he that layeth up treasure for himself, and is not rich toward God."*

Be mindful of who has blessed you and what *his* priorities are, in order that he may use you to fulfill *his* purpose.

The most common form of giving for most Christians is through our offerings and tithes. The tithe, which literally means 10 percent, was required to be given as a reminder to the Israelites of all that God had provided for them. They were instructed to give him the first fruits, the best of their crops before they took any, and to do so with a thankful heart for his provisions. These also provided for the needs of the priests, religious feasts, poor, orphans, and the widows. Offerings were gifts shared based on God's leading and any additional resources that were available. Today these same needs exist, as does our calling to give generously from what we have already received. There are several passages that address this specific area and are important to understand.

- *Proverbs 3:9, 10 KJV Honour the LORD with thy substance, and with the firstfruits of all thine increase: so shall thy barns be filled with plenty, and thy presses shall burst out with new wine.*
- *Leviticus 27:30 KJV And all the tithe of the land, whether of the seed of the land, or of the fruit of the tree, is the LORD's: it is holy unto the LORD.*
- *Acts 20:35 And I have been a constant example of how you can help those in need by working hard. You should remember the words of the Lord Jesus: "It is more blessed to give than to receive."*
- *James 2:14-17 What good is it, dear brothers and sisters, if you say you have faith but don't show it by your actions? Can that kind of faith save anyone? Suppose you see a brother or sister who has no food or clothing, and you say, "Good-bye and have a good day; stay warm and eat well" - but then you don't give that person any food or clothing. What good does that do? So you see, faith by itself isn't enough. Unless it produces good deeds, it is dead and useless.*
- *Matthew 6:1-4 "Watch out! Don't do your good deeds publicly, to be admired by others, for you will lose the reward from your Father in heaven. When you give to someone in need, don't do as the hypocrites do - blowing trumpets in the synagogues and streets to call attention to their acts of charity! I tell you the truth, they have received all the reward they will ever get. But when you give to someone in need, don't let your left hand know what your right hand is doing. Give your gifts in private, and your Father, who sees everything, will reward you."*
- *2 Corinthians 9:7 KJV Every man according as he purposeth in his heart, so let him give; not grudgingly, or of necessity: for God loveth a cheerful giver.*

God calls us to give to him first, not if we have anything left over, understanding that it is better to give than to receive. Our giving provides for the needs of our spiritual leaders which allow them to devote their time to instruct and shepherd the congregations. We must first meet any physical needs before we can address someone's spiritual needs. We should practice humility in our giving, guarding our intentions, and always give with a cheerful heart, thankful for all that he has provided.

Jesus emphasizes that his desire for us is to have a heart that is willing to share everything. *Mark 12:41-44 Jesus sat down near the collection box in the Temple and watched as the crowds dropped in their money. Many rich people put in large amounts. Then a poor widow came and dropped in two small coins. Jesus called his disciples to him and said, "I tell you the truth, this poor widow has given more than all the others who are making contributions. For they gave a tiny part of their surplus, but she, poor as she is, has given everything she had to live on."*

This well known account of the widow offering all that she had points us to Christ and the ultimate sacrifice he made for us. **Jesus is our standard.** As a follower of Christ we look at his example to model our lives after, ready to sacrifice everything as we share his love with the world, and bring glory to God the Father. Your sacrifice might be two copper pennies. It could be helping someone who's been through a trial that you have walked through yourself. Maybe it's spending an afternoon comforting someone who has experienced a loss or is lonely. It might be watching the neighbor's kids or volunteering at a food bank. It could involve sending a note of encouragement to someone whom God has brought to your mind, or giving them a call. Perhaps God has blessed you with some unexpected income, possibly intended to be shared with others as you hear of a need. And maybe . . . just maybe, it is to teach Sunday school to a group of seventh grade boys! In each and every one of these situations, whatever God calls you to do, the Holy Spirit will use your obedience to impact lives for eternity.

You're "everything" is limitless and might look different from day to day. It will involve giving of your finances, time, and talents. It will require you to remember that everything you receive is from God.

When he increases your income in the form of a raise or bonus at work, an inheritance or an investment profit, how do you spend that? Do you need that bigger house, newer car, nicer stuff, or more junk for your kids to have to go through after you have died?! None of that is going with you. Not that we shouldn't upgrade or move as needed, or be able to enjoy what he provides. **Do you prayerfully consider what you are doing with all of your resources, and what his purpose is for giving them to you, before you invest them**?

Consider the additional time he has blessed you with as that has increased, whether through retirement, a period in between jobs, less of a commute time, or having been in lock down mode. Why did he give you that time? What does he want you to pursue? As I have mentioned, the circumstances of this past year have provided me with an opportunity to spend a great deal of time reflecting and examining my life that I wouldn't have had otherwise. What began with anxiety, uncertainty, and a lot of frustration in March, accompanied by an attitude that it could be the worst year ever, has turned out to be completely different. We have received so many blessings as God has provided and surpassed any need we have had, and allowed for an abundance of time with him, family, friends, and introspection.

I understand that money, possessions and time can be considered private matters between you, your spouse, your family, and God. And yet, as he desires for us to grow in our maturity in every area, and to follow his will, **not ours**, he knows that we can't do it on our own. He calls for us to seek wise counsel from others in our decision making, as well as to hold one another accountable, to encourage and sharpen one another, helping us to remain on the right path. These two verses emphasize the necessity of having friends whose wise counsel you trust, and who you are willing to be accountable to.

- *Proverbs 15:22 Plans go wrong for lack of advice; many advisers bring success.*
- *Proverbs 27:17 As iron sharpens iron, so a friend sharpens a friend.*

How many failures and heartaches over the span of our lives could have been avoided if we had truly been seeking God's will first in our life, and by asking our brothers and sisters to be in prayer, offering insights, and holding us to what God desires for us? These are the friendships that you need to cultivate as you seek to wisely invest in his kingdom.

There isn't a gold star chart for what you give or the time you invest, but there is something much better in store. God longs for the desires of your heart to line up with his desires knowing that when that occurs, you won't be thinking about what you are giving up or missing out on in this world. As you look upward and gaze at all of those treasures you are storing in heaven, you will be filled with eternal joy, and will experience a peace and contentment like none you have ever felt before. *Psalms 1:1-3 KJV Blessed is the man that walketh not in the counsel of the ungodly, nor standeth in the way of sinners, nor sitteth in the seat of the scornful. But **his delight is in the law of the LORD**; and in his law doth he meditate day and night. And he shall be like a tree planted by the rivers of water, that bringeth forth his fruit in his season; his leaf also shall not wither; and **whatsoever he doeth shall prosper.***

It's interesting to me how the shape of a heart has become the most common symbol that we associate with love. We express our love for someone by drawing a heart, or in this century, using an emoji! Valentine's Day candy comes in a heart shaped box and greeting cards are filled with hearts expressing love and affection. Jewelry is available in a multitude of heart shaped rings, bracelets, and necklaces for every occasion imaginable. Our greatest command is to love, first and foremost God, and then others. We love what our heart desires. **Pursuing** any treasure is **initiated** by our **desire** for acquiring it, followed by our dedication, sacrifice, and commitment to attaining it. *As you see heart shapes throughout your day, be reminded of who you love first, what his desires are for you, and what treasures he is calling you to be committed to pursue.* **What you truly love you will make time for**.

The lyrics to the song "Thank you for giving to the Lord"[10] by Ray Boltz is a powerful reminder of how God will use us as we love him, love others, and pursue the desires of his heart. It gets my allergies going every time I hear it . . . producing a few tears of thankfulness for those who have given of themselves and poured into my life.

"I dreamed I went to heaven and you were there with me, We walked upon the streets of gold beside the crystal sea. We heard the angels singing then someone called your name, You turned and saw this young man and he was smiling as he came.

He said friend you may not know me now and then he said but wait, You used to teach my Sunday school when I was only eight. And every week you would say a prayer before the class would start. And one day when you said that prayer I asked Jesus in my heart.

Then another man stood before you and said remember the time, A missionary came to your church and his pictures made you cry. You didn't have much money but you gave it all away. Jesus took that gift you gave and that's why I'm here today.

One by one they came far as the eye could see, Each life somehow touched by your generosity. Little things that you had done sacrifices made, Unnoticed on the earth in heaven now proclaimed.

And I know that up in heaven you're not supposed to cry, But I am almost sure there were tears in your eyes. As Jesus took your hand and you stood before the Lord, He said, my child look around you for great is your reward.

Thank you for giving to the Lord, I am a life that was changed. Thank you for giving to the Lord, I am so glad you gave."

These are the treasures that I look forward to experiencing in heaven. Not for recognition or out of a sense of pride, but grateful that my obedience and pursuit of eternal treasure has been realized in their life. I experienced an awesome example of this the first year I went to our church camp. I had gone with a friend who had left early and I did not know anyone else. Sensing my home sickness and despair, this counselor made an effort to keep me involved and spent extra time with me that he could have spent with other staff members his own age. He made sure I was not sitting alone in the meetings or by myself during free time.

What I still remember 50 years later are the hours of ping pong we played together that week. I loved ping pong and was pretty competitive. He was good as well, so we had some great games back and forth. As I looked forward to those games and got to know other kids I ended up having an amazing experience and I went back every year, even working as a leader on staff after high school. Looking back, if he had not noticed or made that special effort, I might not have ever wanted to go back to that camp. The camp where I accepted Christ the following summer. The camp where I made friendships that have lasted to this day. The camp where the memories, experiences, and instruction helped shape who I have become, and what I do. He ended up being a youth pastor at a neighboring church that we did many activities with, so I enjoyed continuing our relationship and learning from his example. Unfortunately I never told him of the impact he had on me during that week. I don't know if I will see him before I get to heaven, so I'll thank him now. *Thank you Gary, for giving to the Lord. I am a life that was changed. I am so glad you gave.*

You might not ever know who you have impacted or how your life has made a difference. How one interaction helped change the desires of a heart or influenced someone's perspective, priorities and purpose. **We are simply called to be faithful, to allow the Holy Spirit to lead and direct us, to obediently follow his path, pursuing his desires, for his glory, enriching his kingdom for eternity!**

Then said Jesus unto his disciples, "If any man will come after me, let him deny himself, and take up his cross, and follow me. For whosoever will save his life shall lose it: and whosoever will lose his life for my sake shall find it. For what is a man profited, if he shall gain the whole world, and lose his own soul? Or what shall a man give in exchange for his soul? For the Son of man shall come in the glory of his Father with his angels; and then he shall reward every man according to his works."
Matthew 16:24-27 KJV

Glorifying God in ALL of My Pursuits

I pray that your love will overflow more and more, and that you will keep on growing in knowledge and understanding. For I want you to understand what really matters, so that you may live pure and blameless lives until the day of Christ's return. May you always be filled with the fruit of your salvation - the righteous character produced in your life by Jesus Christ - for this will bring much glory and praise to God. Philippians 1:9-11

Paul addresses the believers in Philippi with thankfulness and joy as he remembers their partnership with him in spreading the Good News of Christ. He encourages them to remain on this path, confident that God will continue his good work in them until it is finished on the day that Jesus returns. He prays that they will be obedient and grow in the characteristics that bring praise to God.   A love that overflows, a continual increase of knowledge, living a life of purity, being blameless, producing fruit as a result of their salvation, and possessing a righteous and excellent character. **To understand what really matters.** Paul knew what was most important in the realm of eternity as he exhorted the Philippians to pursue these attributes for God's glory, **in all they did.**

As followers of Jesus and being conformed daily to his image through our obedience to his plan for our lives, we must comprehend and embrace those last four words. **In all they did.**   Jesus is always being Jesus. That is who he has always been and who he will always be. **Remember, he is our standard.**   His desires must become our desires as we grow in him and remain dedicated to his plan. In all we do. Once more for emphasis . . . **In all we do!** What are the desires of your heart every morning as you rise and go about your day? Do you seek God's direction to lead and guide you as to what his plan is for your day? To show you whom to share his love with? To point out areas you need to be obedient in? How to best spend the time and talents you have been given? Do you ask yourself, "Is what I am investing in today going to have an impact for eternity?" If your standard is Jesus, he has always been about his Father's business, even as a young boy. *Luke 2:49 "But why did you need to search?" he asked. "Didn't you know that I must be in my Father's house?"*

Let's take this concept to the next level and look for a moment at how we invest our "free time." Other names we use might be spare time, down time, leisure time, or my favorite, "me time." That one is usually reserved for moms or dads who stay at home with those sweet, precious, little toddler blessings from God, especially if there is more than one in the house. And if your quiver is full of a few at that age, there is also the mandatory "alone time!" Other areas that fall into this category of free time would be our hobbies, recreational activities, and opportunities for personal enrichment. **We fill this time with what we truly love, what we are passionate about, with what our heart desires**.

Julie loves to retreat to her arts and crafts room. I do not join her there very often unless I am removing a spider or moving a heavy object. I prefer to golf or watch some sort of sporting event, confident that my team will blow another game, and yet I still watch. Our children and grandchildren enjoy music, photography, videography, gaming, theater and many other good and worthwhile interests. Our family enjoys playing table games, going to movies, and travelling together. A few will labor over a jigsaw puzzle, especially during the holidays, working on one for a few days until it is completed and then dump the pieces back into the box. During our dating years I began a tradition of slyly slipping one piece away into my possession so that I could be the one to finish the masterpiece. I've given that up as I have matured a little, but still get blamed when one is missing - even though the tradition has been continued by Dylan. Many people prefer reading, watching TV, hunting, painting, learning a new language - there are so many wonderful and productive ways to fill up our free time.

As you consider glorifying God in all of your pursuits, do not forget that he has given you that "free time." Just like every other perfect gift he gives. Also remember that he gave you the desires and interests that you have. He has designed you to enjoy those gifts, talents, and passions. He simply desires that you pursue them with **his** perspective, priorities and purpose in mind. As you examine your pursuits, ask yourself:

- Do my investments in these areas bring glory to God?
- How does my participation in these influence my witness for Jesus?

Based on your answers to the following questions you can determine if they are worthy of "your" time, if they align with his desires for you, and if they will produce fruit here on earth as well as eternal blessings.

- Do my most important relationships flourish or suffer?
- How much time do I devote?
- How much money do I invest?
- Is my witness for Christ enhanced or hindered?

If we as Christians are about loving God, loving others, and obediently pursuing his desires with all of our heart, soul, and mind, then that must be intertwined through everything we participate in, every area of our life, each and every day. Just like the widow who gave all that she had, God wants every part of us, including our time, to be focused on him. The fact is, it's his already. Ask for the Holy Spirit to lead you in this area and to make it clear how **he** intends for you to be investing **his** time, spending **his** money, using **his** talents, and enjoying **his** hobbies, all for **his** glory. There are hundreds of references throughout the Scriptures that remind us that we are to glorify God in all that we do. Here are just a few.

- *Psalms 115:1 KJV Not unto us, O LORD, not unto us, but unto thy name give glory, for thy mercy, and for thy truth's sake.*
- *Philippians 4:13 For I can do everything through Christ, who gives me strength.*
- *John 15:8 "When you produce much fruit, you are my true disciples. This brings great glory to my Father."*
- *Psalms 86:12 KJV I will praise thee, O Lord my God, with all my heart: and I will glorify thy name for evermore.*

That is our primary purpose here on this earth. In our church growing up we were taught that the chief end of man is to glorify God and enjoy him forever. Sometimes I have to catch myself as I think that eternity will start once we reach heaven. We are part of eternity right now. We have eternal souls. Your forever has already begun. We will fully experience God's glory once we reach heaven, but until then we must fulfill our purpose here on earth. **To glorify God and enjoy him forever**.

"To God be the glory, great things He hath done, so loved he the world that he gave us his Son. Who yielded his life an atonement for sin, and opened the life gate that all my go in.

O perfect redemption, the purchase of blood, to every believer the promise of God. The vilest offender who truly believes, that moment from Jesus a pardon receives.

Great things he hath taught us, great things he hath done, and great our rejoicing through Jesus the Son. But purer, and higher, and greater will be, our wonder, our rapture, when Jesus we see!

Praise the Lord, praise the Lord, let the earth hear his voice! Praise the Lord, praise the Lord, let the people rejoice! O come to the Father, through Jesus the son, And give him the glory, great things he hath done."

This is one of over 8000 hymns written by Fanny Crosby, who wrote her first song at age six! Physically blind all of her life, God's Spirit obviously inspired her insights as these lyrics reveal such profound truths and vision as to her eternal focus, as well as to what ours should be.

Let the whole earth sing to the Lord! Each day proclaim the good news that he saves. Publish his glorious deeds among the nations. Tell everyone about the amazing things he does. Great is the Lord! He is most worthy of praise! He is to be feared above all gods. The gods of other nations are mere idols, but the Lord made the heavens! Honor and majesty surround him; strength and joy fill his dwelling. O nations of the world, recognize the Lord, recognize that the Lord is glorious and strong. Give to the Lord the glory he deserves! Bring your offering and come into his presence. Worship the Lord in all his holy splendor. 1 Chronicles 16:23-29

What You Truly Love You will Make Time for

And I beheld, and I heard the voice of many angels round about the throne and the beasts and the elders: and the number of them was ten thousand times ten thousand, and thousands of thousands; saying with a loud voice, "Worthy is the Lamb that was slain to receive power, and riches, and wisdom, and strength, and honour, and glory, and blessing." And every creature which is in heaven, and on the earth, and under the earth, and such as are in the sea, and all that are in them, heard I saying, "Blessing, and honour, and glory, and power, be unto him that sitteth upon the throne, and unto the Lamb for ever and ever." And the four beasts said, "Amen." And the four and twenty elders fell down and worshiped him that liveth for ever and ever. Revelation 5:11-14 KJV

As we study the visions that John lays out for us in the book of Revelation, his descriptiveness is beyond our comprehension. What a magnificent scene, a throng of millions, a mighty chorus all focused on the one who is worthy. The only one who is worthy - to receive power and riches and wisdom and strength and honor and glory and blessing. This worship in heaven helps us realize how we should devote that same focus to him in all that we do while we are still here on the earth. **He is worthy of our love.**

Every area of our life, only he is worthy to lead. The use of any talent and blessing that we have received, only he is worthy to lead. Each relationship we enjoy, only he is worthy to lead. Any situation where we need guidance, only he is worthy to lead. This picture of the throng of millions offering their worship and praise to the Lamb on his throne for ever and ever is evidence of **who they truly love**.

As this book comes to a close we need to ask ourselves, is there evidence in each area of our life that shows we believe that he alone is worthy to lead us? Are we willing to surrender all, to trust and obey him in everything, and to fix our eyes on Jesus alone to plan and guide our path forward? Do we truly love and desire all that he asks of us, all that he commands? The lyrics in this Keith Green classic "To Obey is Better than Sacrifice"[11] serve as a sobering reminder of what Christ desires, and should give us pause as we examine the condition of our hearts.

"To obey is better than sacrifice, I don't need your money, I want your life. And I hear you say that I'm coming back soon, but you act like I'll never return.

Well you speak of grace and my love so sweet, how you thrive on milk but reject my meat. And I can't help weeping of how it will be, if you keep on ignoring my words.

Well you pray to prosper and succeed, but your flesh is something I just can't feed.

To obey is better than sacrifice, I want more than Sunday and Wednesday nights. Cause if you can't come to me every day, then don't bother coming at all.

To obey is better than sacrifice, I want hearts of fire not your prayers of ice. And I'm coming back quickly to give back to you, according to what you have done."

We will all be required to give an account for what we have done, or what we have not done. Good or Bad. Right or Wrong. That is God's promise to us, to help us keep our focus on him and what matters for eternity. *Romans 2:6-8 He will judge everyone according to what they have done. He will give eternal life to those who keep on doing good, seeking after the glory and honor and immortality that God offers. But he will pour out his anger and wrath on those who live for themselves, who refuse to obey the truth and instead live lives of wickedness.*

As I mentioned in the opening chapter, the circumstances of this past year have caused me to contemplate the questions above very personally. To examine the evidence of my life. To really be honest about whom I truly love and what my heart desires, knowing that I will be called to give an account for my decisions. The Holy Spirit has led me to **reflect** on my perspective, priorities, and purpose. To **inspect** each area and evaluate if any changes needed to be made. To take the steps necessary to **correct** whatever was not focused on eternal matters. And as a result, to ultimately **connect** with God on a level that he has always intended for me, while being able to glorify him in the process. This must be an ongoing examination!

My hope is that you have been encouraged and challenged by these words, and inspired to examine your life and your remaining days in a similar manner. My prayer as you reflect, inspect, and correct, is that you will then be able to connect with God the Father on a deeper level, that you will desire to continue to develop your relationship with Christ the Son as he instructs, and that you will experience the Holy Spirit's leading in a new and profound way for the rest of your life.

In the field of Experiential Learning (a fancy name for the team building programs that I lead) as we finish the day and are processing the experience, there is a phrase that is commonly used to help participants personalize their experience. **What. So What. Now What**. This reflective model was first developed by John Driscoll in 1994.[12] The "What" refers to the activities and interactions that took place. The "So What" pertains to any observations, lessons learned, or "Ah ha" moments. The "Now What" is the transference of the experience and applications back to your life - the "Where do I go from here," and "How can I apply this moving forward" questions. The proper facilitation of this allows for the participants to discuss and explore what their personal takeaways are, instead of being told what they were supposed to learn, thus making them more likely to take them to heart and implement them as desired. Each person might have a different take or have had different insights on what they need to apply in their own lives.

I encourage you to not skip or ignore the "Now What" stage as it relates to your relationship with God. **We all need to be continually seeking the Holy Spirit's guidance and responding to his prompting as it occurs.** If you sense the need for a minor adjustment or are ready for a major overhaul in any of the areas that have been discussed, prayerfully seek his guidance and let him lead you back in the right direction. Do not put this off or downplay the significance of what you know in your heart to be necessary. *Joshua 24:15 KJV And if it seem evil unto you to serve the LORD, choose you this day whom ye will serve; whether the gods which your fathers served that were on the other side of the flood, or the gods of the Amorites, in whose land ye dwell: but as for me and my house, we will serve the LORD.*

Choose today whom you will serve. Remember, you will be called to give an account for your life in Christ. What you truly loved. What you made time for. Heed the warning of Jesus in Revelations to the angel of the church in Laodicea, and ask yourself "Is that describing me? Is that my church?"

*Revelation 3:14-22 "Write this letter to the angel of the church in Laodicea. This is the message from the one who is the Amen - the faithful and true witness, the beginning of God's new creation: I know all the things you do, that you are neither hot nor cold. I wish that you were one or the other! But since you are like lukewarm water, neither hot nor cold, **I will** spit you out of my mouth! You say, 'I am rich. I have everything I want. I don't need a thing!' And you don't realize that you are wretched and miserable and poor and blind and naked. So I advise you to buy gold from me - gold that has been purified by fire. Then you will be rich. Also buy white garments from me so you will not be shamed by your nakedness, and ointment for your eyes so you will be able to see. I correct and discipline everyone I love. So be diligent and turn from your indifference. Look! I stand at the door and knock. If you hear my voice and open the door, I will come in, and we will share a meal together as friends. Those who are victorious will sit with me on my throne, just as I was victorious and sat with my Father on his throne. Anyone with ears to hear must listen to the Spirit and understand what he is saying to the churches."*

I pray that this description does not apply to you, and yet if it does, it is not too late. He is pleading once again for you to return to your first love. God is a just and righteous God who will eventually unleash his judgement on us all. Fortunately he is also a loving, gracious, and merciful God who wants no one to perish or wander away from him. He is constantly calling to us, warning us, pleading with us, as he disciplines the ones he loves. Notice the bold words in this passage. **I will**. He has not done it yet. He is waiting. But he is getting ready or he would not warn us. I cannot think of anything that tastes appealing when it is lukewarm. We ice our drinks to make them cold, heat our soup, and warm up our coffee to enjoy a hot beverage. What love he has for us. What patience with us. That foul taste of our **apathy and indifference** is just sitting there in his mouth.

His concern was not that they were murderous, adulterous or wicked people. **This was a group who believed in him**. Who followed him. Who went to the pot lucks. Sang in the choir. Taught Sunday school. Ministered to the community. I assume that they were very involved and passionate at one point. He is warning them to return to him, to get back on the path he had designed for them. They were being choked by the thorns and did not even realize it. He longed for his desires to once again be their desires, not the worldly wealth or provisions they had pursued and were enjoying, that will not last. **Have you forgotten who has given you everything?** Do you hold it all in your open hand for him to use for his glory? What he offers is eternal. He pleads for them to repent and turn back to him, as he pleads with us when we fall away or forget what is most important. He demands we give him everything and yet in return, he blesses us with so much more than we could have hoped for. **His blessings are not temporal**. Imagine dining with Jesus in heaven on his throne forever. Open your eyes, hear his voice, fling open that door. Let it fly off its hinges! Listen to what he is saying to you and respond to his call while you still can.

Let me speak to a specific group for a moment, as my heart has always loved ministry involving young people. Teenagers. Young adults. It is time to stand up and be counted, to make your beliefs publicly known for all to see, fully committed to your Savior and Lord. Do not continue as babies in your faith, just being content with your salvation, but rather pursue his knowledge and wisdom so that you may grow your faith and be strong in the Lord. Guard your heart above all else, as it will determine the course for your life. Ignore what the world throws at you and tempts you with, trying to convince you of its importance. Instead you must **Stand out** from the world as a follower of Christ, and be his ambassador as you go throughout your day. Show those around you his love and kindness in all that you do. Seek his plan for your life. Ask him to make his desires your desires and pursue them obediently as he leads. You can make a difference. Right now. Today. **God has a plan for your life**. *Joshua 1:7 Be strong and very courageous. Be careful to obey all the instructions Moses gave you. Do not deviate from them, turning either to the right or to the left. Then you will be successful in everything you do.*

Do not delay seeking his direction until you have graduated, gone to college, chosen a career, or started a family. Your life is already happening and he has a purpose for whatever chapter you are currently in. I was 18 just a few short years ago. In the blink of an eye you will be looking back on your life. **Make it count for Christ and his Kingdom today.** *1 Timothy 4:11, 12 Teach these things and insist that everyone learn them. Don't let anyone think less of you because you are young. Be an example to all believers in what you say, in the way you live, in your love, your faith, and your purity.*

The Bible is full of young men and women who were obedient to God's calling at an early age, willing to walk down his path. They were blessed and used mightily for his purpose and glory. Joseph, David, Miriam, Esther, Mary. These are just a few examples of who God used in amazing ways. Do not ignore today what he is calling you to do. He knows the impact your witness will have as you study his word, stay in close fellowship with other believers, ask for his guidance, and seek his will and his desires.

You are in a battle for your soul. For your friend's soul. For your classmates' soul. For your teammates' soul. For your teacher's soul. For your neighbor's soul. Even for the soul of the person who is not kind, or mistreats you. They do not even know they are under assault as they wander aimlessly in the dark, seeking purpose and direction from sources that will never satisfy them. You know the truth of who can provide the life and fulfillment they are seeking. **You can make a difference.** Prepare for this fight daily by dressing in God's armor so you will win this victory.

Ephesians 6:10-18 A final word: Be strong in the Lord and in his mighty power. Put on all of God's armor so that you will be able to stand firm against all strategies of the devil. For we are not fighting against flesh and blood enemies, but against evil rulers and authorities of the unseen world, against mighty powers in this dark world, and against evil spirits in the heavenly places. ***Therefore, put on every piece of God's armor so you will be able to resist the enemy in the time of evil. Then after the battle you will still be standing firm***. *Stand your ground, putting on the belt of truth and the body armor of God's* *righteousness. For shoes, put on the peace that comes from the Good News so that you will be fully prepared. In addition to all of these, hold up the shield of faith to stop the fiery arrows of the devil. Put on salvation as your helmet, and take the sword of the Spirit, which is the word of God. Pray in the Spirit at all times and on every occasion. Stay alert and be persistent in your prayers for all believers everywhere.*

Believe his promises. Obey his wisdom and instruction. Live out his desires as they are better than anything else that you can ever imagine. More satisfying than any temporal treasure that the world has to offer you. Remember that you have a personal relationship with Almighty God and you have access to all of his power. Claim it now! **You will never be disappointed in what he has promised to deliver.** May God bless and strengthen you as you answer his call.

Earlier in this chapter I talked about the "Now What" concept of processing information that has been received and experienced. The "Where do I go from here," and "How can I apply this moving forward" questions. The need to grasp the importance of continually seeking the Holy Spirit's guidance and responding to his prompting as he leads. To not put off or downplay the significance of changes that you know in your heart are necessary.

I have always been a big believer in the importance of setting goals and the benefits that they hold for keeping us focused on what we want to accomplish. These chapter titles started out on a sheet of paper 35 years ago as areas that I wanted to focus on throughout my life, with goals that I wanted to achieve. Now I know that some people do not like the concept of goal setting and feel that it is too restrictive or demanding. They might get discouraged if they do not succeed in reaching it, or dislike the pressure it brings. However, many of our successes would not have been realized without designing and following a plan. When you "Fail to plan, you plan to fail,"[13] is a Benjamin Franklin quote that is often used, simple yet true. Do you ever find yourself drifting, not sure what direction to go in or how to get there? It's hard to be successful when you just wing it.

The Scriptures are full of verses that pertain to the importance of planning and goal setting. These are just a few.

- Luke 14:28 *"But don't begin until you count the cost. For who would begin construction of a building without first calculating the cost to see if there is enough money to finish it?"*
- Proverbs 1:23 *Come and listen to my counsel. I'll share my heart with you and make you wise.*
- Proverbs 13:16 *Wise people think before they act; fools don't - and even brag about their foolishness.*
- Proverbs 24:27 KJV *Prepare thy work without, and make it fit for thyself in the field; and afterwards build thine house.*

Setting goals is imperative as you prepare and train, hoping to receive the victor's crown. Rafer Johnson[14] won the gold medal for the decathlon at the 1960 Olympics. This is a competition which combines 10 track and field events over a two day period, and the winner is recognized as "The world's greatest athlete" because of the variety of feats that they had to master in order to win. He understood as well as anyone what he needed to be focused on. He knew about the hours of training, preparation, and sacrifice that were invested in becoming a champion, and were required to reach his goal.

I heard a story that years later he was speaking to a room full of Olympic athletes who were training for the upcoming games. All of them were very accomplished and successful, the top athletes in their sport. He began by asking them if they had specific goals that they had set for their performance. Every hand in the room went up. He then asked if those goals had been written down, had been stated so that they could be a reminder of what was being pursued. Every hand in the room went up. Lastly, he asked how many of those world class athletes had that list of goals with them at that moment. None of the hands were raised. This story has always highlighted to me how crucial it is for us to not only have goals and to be reminded of them on a regular basis, but to also evaluate them often and keep them in sight in order to achieve them.

I would like to share a few thoughts that have proven valuable on this topic for me and our family over the years that I have gleaned from a variety of sources. Hopefully they will provide you with some insights and ideas as you personalize what God has in mind for you. As your personality, gifts, and path might differ from mine, I encourage you to allow the Holy Spirit to help you examine and design the goals and format that will best enable you to run your race.

We remember that Jesus got up early, went to a quiet place and prayed. This is how I would begin your planning and goal setting process, as it is always a great idea to start by talking to the expert and getting His wisdom. If possible, go someplace other than your normal setting and avoid distractions. If you can get away for a night or weekend, even better. Don't rush this process. If you're married, include your spouse in this process. Invest significant time as you examine your heart in any of these, or other areas, asking the Holy Spirit to reveal his perspective, priority, and purpose for you. *Psalms 46:10 KJV Be still, and know that I am God: I will be exalted among the heathen, I will be exalted in the earth.* If you can't get away, just lock the kids in a room with some ice cream and get to work. Just kidding. Once they've gone to bed or early in the morning are usually excellent opportunities that will allow you to give this ample time. It might take a few sessions to put your plan together - no need to rush.

Over the past 35 years I have accomplished some of the goals that I established. Some I have not. Many that are related to my spiritual growth are ongoing and will be for the rest of my life. I have adjusted a few as circumstances change. Being realistic is important so that you will not get discouraged or give up. Remember, you are evaluating your progress periodically, and can set the bar higher or lower at any point, as needed. These do not have to be written in stone, do or die, succeed or fail experiences. There is no expiration date or deadline. You can start over or keep plugging away. Just don't give up. Press on!

For several years I have led a ski camp and taught many kids and adults who were beginners. I am not an expert or certified instructor, but I have been able to help everyone pick it up and get down a green run (the easiest slope after the practice hill) by the end of the first day. That is always my goal and I encourage them as they struggle initially, to hang in there, to not get frustrated, that they will figure it out.

If you've ever skied you know the joy of cramming your feet into those 1959 model boots, feeling like one of Cinderella's step sisters, desperately trying to make that glass slipper fit. Or the ease with which you carry your skis and poles out to the slopes while walking in those same boots, usually up 3 or 4 flights of stairs - made even more memorable if you're carrying a second or third set for your children - who compliantly walk beside you, quietly, opening doors, never dropping a glove, and following your instructions to stay out of the snow, especially the yellow spots. You have experienced the difficulty of figuring out how to slide those new 6 foot feet you are maneuvering around on a slippery surface, realizing that your glass slippers that took 30 minutes to try on are 2 sizes too small. Throw in the perils of your first chair lift adventure, getting stuck on that magic carpet for 15 minutes, cold, wind, and snow, a runny nose, as well as the challenges of avoiding the overly aggressive 5 year olds that keep zig zagging past you, and it is then that you realize what a wonderful idea it was to learn how to ski. Very similar to the relaxing, first snorkeling experience you had in the warm, aqua colored waters of the Cayman Islands!

A few years ago, I was able to share this experience with my brother in law, Tunde. He had never been before and so I offered to help him learn. He was gung ho, ready for anything, listened attentively and did everything that I asked him to do. There was one issue we faced that I had never experienced before, and that was that the snow was hard, icy and very unforgiving. It resulted in an increase of speed, allowed for less control while attempting to turn, and made it extremely difficult to come to a smooth stop. Not ideal circumstances for anyone, especially a beginner.

After the third, fourth, tenth time he fell - I might have lost track, I decided that it would be easier for me to just help him up each time instead of going through the chore of popping off his skis and then having to get those Cinderella slippers locked back in each time. I might not have thought this strategy through well enough, as he was considerably heavier than most 10-13 year olds that I was accustomed to helping. Just picture if you can, one grown man hugging another, both on skis, attempting to regain their balance and stance, on an icy slope with those pesky 5 year old terrors flying by.

After the third, fourth, fifteenth time I had picked him up - I definitely lost track - I was exhausted, my back was sore and muscles ached that I never knew I had. Tunde was bruised and battered but still determined to learn, confident that progress was being made, so we pressed on.

After the . . . . . ok, you've got the idea. Let's just say that I picked Tunde up so many times that morning, wrapping my arms around him over and over, my face buried in his neck, that I can still smell the cologne he was wearing, now thirteen years later. Through great effort and persistence by the end of the morning he had figured it out and made it down that practice slope without falling. After lunch we decided that a ride to the top of the slopes in the gondola - which he had never done before -in order to see the view and take some pictures was what he would enjoy the most. We did not get down a green slope that day but we experienced something so much better, as we were able to stand at the top of that mountain, surrounded by God's beauty, majesty, and glory, soaking in just a taste of who he is.

Sometimes you will need to make adjustments to your goals and that is fine. You might need to re-evaluate the reality of some based on your situation and whether that goal is beneficial or not. Unmet goals are not the end of the world. Maybe a different one will lead you to see God's majestic creation on a mountain top with your brother in a way that you never have before. Allow the Holy Spirit's guidance to lead you to establish helpful and reachable goals that will influence and strengthen every area of your life, keeping you focused on his eternal plan for his glory.

I suggest that you break down your goals into three time frames. Remember this is an example that I like. You might find something more effective for you.

- Short term: One month goals
- Long term: One year goals
- Epitaph: What's on your tombstone

It's said that if you can maintain a routine for three to four weeks it will be more likely to become a regular habit. This is the importance of short term goals - to get the process started that will develop the practice and lead to consistency and dedication.

They should be attainable but require commitment and faithfulness each day, in order to be established. The long term goal might be an extension of a short term one, or a result that you desire to observe over a longer period of time. These should all be specific and able to be measured as you evaluate their effectiveness in your walk. Finally, I would suggest you write an epitaph, a short reminder of what you would like your legacy to have been. The impact you have made. I have offered some examples below on the areas that we have discussed. These are just some basics to get you thinking - you need to personalize and flesh out your own ideas as the Spirit leads. As you focus on goals that will lead to spiritual growth and an eternal focus, some will be easier to come up with, but all will play a worthwhile role. The harder we work at anything, the greater the sense of accomplishment we will gain once we've achieved it.

Relationship with God
Short term: Bible reading and prayer; verse memorization
Long term: Read a certain number of chapters; memorize a certain number of verses
Epitaph: "Above all else, he desired what mattered to God"

Relationship with Spouse
Short term: Pray and read the Bible together; weekly date; level 4 communication
Long term: Experience something new together; annual getaway to recalibrate
Epitaph: "He loved as Christ loves"

Relationship with Children
Short term: Train for Godliness with specifics; 1 on 1 time each week
Long term: Discover and help develop what makes them tick; annual getaway
Epitaph: "He taught us well"

Fellowship with Believers
Short term: Church and small group weekly; weekly lunch to encourage someone
Long term: Identify a ministry to help in; annual getaway with other believers
Epitaph: "He served others with all of his heart"

Evangelism and Discipleship
Short term: Pray for someone to share the Gospel with and disciple; respond to his call
Long term: Look for weekly opportunities to share and to disciple someone regularly
Epitaph: "He made an eternal difference for many"

Laboring for God's Glory
Short term: Focus on God's plan - be an example;   limit time away from the family
Long term: Have you made a difference in other's lives; put others needs first
Epitaph: "He worked heartily as unto the Lord"

Honoring His Temple
Short term: Daily exercise; good diet; is what you fill your mind with Godly?
Long term: Weight and exercise benchmarks; TV and other consumption down
Epitaph: "He allowed God to live on his throne"

Storing Treasures in Heaven
Short term: Give to God first; evaluate the need before a purchase; eternal focus
Long term: Use all gifts for his glory; find opportunities to share what he has given
Epitaph: "His mansion in heaven is full"

Glorifying God in All Pursuits
Short term: How does he wants to use your talents; opportunity to teach skill to others
Long term: Pursue interests with his plan in mind; use for his purposes.
Epitaph: "Lives were changed for God's glory"

You can simplify these goals to bullet points and put them on an index card to carry in your wallet or purse - or fanny pack - if you still have one of those. Or put them into that electronic device that appears to be surgically attached to us everywhere we go.
That is the only reason to be constantly looking at your phone!
Having the Bible app also brings the word of God with you wherever you go and serves as the best resource in determining God's direction and wisdom. Memorizing verses that relate to a

goal that you have set will help you keep it at the forefront of your thoughts and desires. A few examples would be the following.

Avoiding Temptation	*Psalms 119:11 KJV Thy word have I hid in mine heart, that I might not sin against thee.*
Studying the Bible	*Joshua 1:8 KJV This book of the law shall not depart out of thy mouth; but thou shalt meditate therein day and night, that thou mayest observe to do according to all that is written therein: for then thou shalt make thy way prosperous, and then thou shalt have good success.*
Obeying Parents	*Colossians 3:20 KJV Children, obey your parents in all things; for this is well pleasing unto the Lord.*
Putting God First	*Proverbs 3:5, 6 KJV Trust in the LORD with all thine heart; and lean not unto thine own understanding. In all thy ways acknowledge him, and he shall direct thy paths.*

What you truly love you will make time for. Have I said that enough yet? Is it etched into your brain? Are you guarding your heart above all else, knowing that your heart directs and determines the course of your life? Do you realize that you pursue the desires of your heart? Are they God's desires? Do you love what God loves? Do you make time for what God desires? **Are you committed to doing whatever it takes to love and serve him?** I have been told by those closest to me that my sense of humor has a tendency to beat something to death. Even if it is not funny to them at first, they eventually are worn down and find humor in the constant drip drip drip of my repetitiveness. So let me ask once more . . . . What are you focused on? Which direction are you headed in? **Whose perspective, priorities and purpose are you seeking?**

Let's return to that waiting room in the doctor's office. If you had received that prognosis informing you that you only had 3 months left to live, what items would be on your bucket list? How would you spend the time you had left? Some might want to visit an exotic destination and enjoy the warmth of the sun and sounds of the ocean one last time. Others might choose a majestic mountain range, to feel the cool, crisp air and admire its beauty and splendor. A few might opt for something exciting and daring that they had not mustered up the courage for earlier in life, maybe skydiving or scuba diving with sharks. Maybe it would involve returning to a special location that held sentimental value. Whom would you seek out and what would be your focus? Would your final pursuits be temporal in nature, providing one last memory, smile, thrill or goodbye? Or would your bucket list items serve an eternal purpose, pointing others to Christ? Your eyes fixed on what is yet to come in your heavenly home, engulfed with a peace and joy that passes all understanding, bringing all glory to God?

We have all received that terminal prognosis; we just don't know our length of time. Moses encourages us in *Psalms 90:12 KJV So teach us to number our days, that we may **apply our hearts unto wisdom**.* Guard your heart above all else. Is the course of your life following what God has planned for you? Do you love God with all of your heart, soul and mind? Do you love your neighbor as yourself?

We are all at varying stages along our path and though our journeys may be different, our destination is the same. If you are a committed believer, seeking God's plan and obedient to his call, stay the course. With humility keep your eyes on him and finish the race with a sprint to the finish. If you are a newer Christian just getting started in your relationship, seek out someone who can guide you and help you to understand what his plan is for you. Keep the passion you have for this new life burning hot, pressing forward, focused on all that he has in store for you. If you've gotten off his path, you can still turn around. Look up - he will guide you back. Peter walked on the waves when he kept his gaze on Jesus. Sometimes we don't realize we are lost or sinking, we just can't see it. Remember, He can pluck you out of *any* circumstance. Even a nasty old pig sty. Just come home. Don't be afraid. You will be welcomed with open arms. **That is what he desires**. He will leave the other 99 to bring the 1 lost sheep home. If you are not a believer, it is not too late to make that decision. It's your choice. **He loves you more than anyone ever can**. That is why he sent Jesus. To bring you peace and joy on earth and to give you an eternal home with him in heaven. To continue on his path, growing to your full maturity in Christ.

- Those who know God have great **energy** for God.
- Those who know God have great **thoughts** of God.
- Those who know God show great **boldness** for God.
- Those who know God have great **contentment** in God.

Julie has always had a fascination with clouds. She loves to draw, paint and photograph them. She is constantly looking up as we are on a walk, sitting in our yard, or driving along a highway peering out the window. I have often teased her about the formations that she sees and the awe with how she describes them, with a wonder that I have not been able to grasp. They just look like pillows or cotton balls to me, a curse of my lack of creativity I guess. I was never one to lie on the grass as a child and look up pretending a cloud was an elephant or a car; it was too itchy and I just wanted to play. I have taken a few photographs from a plane as the clouds drift by below with mountains, lakes, farmland, or cities as their backdrop, many miles beneath them. The view from above allows me to grasp a tiny bit of God's perspective of how he sees so much that we cannot, and provides comfort and confidence in his plan for me. The most animated Julie gets is when a sunset streams through the clouds, producing radiant beams of light. So majestic, it is hard to turn your eye away from that scene. But even that does not compare with the wonder that all will see when Jesus returns, his radiance exploding through the heavens. I think that is what Julie has been doing all these years, looking up to see him as he bursts through those clouds! Needless to say, I have been looking up more often - I am still just seeing pillows and cotton balls - but my gaze is eagerly awaiting his arrival.

Revelation 1:7, 8 Look! He comes with the clouds of heaven. And everyone will see him, even those who pierced him. And all the nations of the world will mourn for him. Yes! Amen! "I am the Alpha and the Omega - the beginning and the end," says the Lord God. "I am the one who is, who always was, and who is to still come - the Almighty One!"

What you truly love you will make time for. What do you desire? Who do you desire? His desire is for us to be ready and waiting, looking above. Love him. Love others. Look upward, focused on his creation, majesty, power, and glory. Make time to gaze heavenward, hoping and longing for that day with great anticipation and confidence. **Be prepared for his return**!

"Blessed Assurance" is another of Fanny Crosby's amazing songs of assurance, praise and anticipation of living in the house of the Lord forever!

> "Blessed assurance, Jesus is mine, O what a foretaste of glory divine. Heir of salvation, purchase of God, born of his Spirit, washed in his blood.
>
> Perfect submission, perfect delight, visions of rapture now burst on my sight. Angels descending, bring from above, echoes of mercy, whispers of love.
>
> Perfect submission, all is at rest, I in my Savior am happy and blessed. Watching and waiting, looking above, filled with his goodness, lost in his love.
>
> This is my story, this is my song. Praising my Savior, all the day long. This is my story, this is my song. Praising my Savior, all the day long."

The one thing I ask of the Lord - the thing I seek most - is to live in the house of the Lord all the days of my life, delighting in the Lord's perfections and meditating in his Temple. Psalms 27:4

A Stick, a Rock, and a Box

Whatever is good and perfect is a gift coming down to us from God our Father, who created all the lights in the heavens. He never changes or casts a shifting shadow. He chose to give birth to us by giving us his true word. And we, out of all creation, became his prized possession. James 1:17, 18

A few years ago in the fall when Dylan was eight, he began contemplating what he would like for Christmas. As most boys that age will do, he kept adding to his wish list as the next best thing would appear in a commercial, a new gaming character would be released, or a friend would mention what they were hoping to receive. It was actually a pretty small and manageable list, but as it grew I felt inclined to bring the bigger picture back into focus for him. As a "Get off my lawn!" old school guy, I had to make it clear to him that based on **my** childhood experiences, he did not need all of those things in order to be entertained or happy. And so the phrase was born.

"When I was your age, all we had to play with was a stick, a rock, and a box . . . . and we liked it!" This was repeated quite often after he would make the mistake of pondering over another gift idea within range of my hearing. It got to the point where I would say, "You know Dylan, when I was your age . . ." and he would respond, "Yeah, I know Grandpa: a stick, a rock, and a box. Whatever!" As my tendency to beat something to death played out with this mantra, he would give a sigh, smirk a little, then make a smart alec comment about how he was glad that life was better now, or would question how we could have ever survived in the "olden days."

As the magical 25th day of December approached, a "brilliant" idea popped into my head of how I could make a humorous point to an eight year old concerning the importance of enjoying the simpler things in life. I found a box bigger than any other gift that was under the tree (it probably could have held a 1965 RCA TV console - just so you can get an accurate picture of the scene that was about to unfold). Wrapped nicely and placed front and center before anyone had risen on Christmas morning, I waited for Dylan's arrival, intending to give him a hint as to what to expect, if he had not already comprehended the joke before opening it. On the box I had written, "Merry Christmas, Dylan.

Love Grandpa – 1968." (The year when I was eight) That would make it pretty obvious to anyone what was inside, right??!!

In some other universe I guess, I imagined an eight year old would calmly approach this monstrosity of a gift on Christmas morning, carefully and thoughtfully read the note, appreciate the humor, and enjoy a good laugh. After all, our routine was to have some brunch, let the kids go through their stockings and then calmly take turns opening gifts, after we had read the account of Jesus's birth. Now before you judge me on my parenting skills and what a cruel thing this was to do to a child, I'll admit - I did not think it all the way through. I had failed to see an alternate reality and was quite shocked to see the different direction that unfolded, immediately realizing my mistake, while helplessly trying to prepare him for a major disappointment.

As that eight year old boy bounded down the stairs brimming with an eagerness and anticipation that only a Christmas morning can bring, he stopped in his tracks as his eye caught sight of the box. Realizing it had not been there the night before, he quickly looked to see whose name was on it. And then, in an instant, without grasping the reference to 1968 or recalling the past few months of what I had been pounding into his head, something came over him. He had never displayed this behavior before, and I have never seen it since. It can only be described as a crazed, maniacal excitement as he tore through that paper and ripped open the box. He hadn't asked for anything that would come in such a large package, so in a matter of seconds his mind raced furiously, delirious as to what it could possibly be, what wonderful surprise awaited . . . . while in the background I heard Julie quietly say, "This isn't going to be good."

So the good news is, Dylan is now 14 and still lives with us. I would like to say that when he peered into that box it contained something greater than he could have ever imagined, that he was thrilled beyond words, more grateful for a gift than he had ever been, and that he was brought to tears over the joy of what he had received. But we all know what was in that box . . . . they were the items that I grew up playing with; a stick, and a rock. In a moment his jubilation was replaced by the sad realization of an unmet expectation that his mysterious treasure was not to be claimed.

As he was processing this unexpected development, fighting back tears of disappointment, I felt horrible and apologized for my poor attempt at humor, hoping he wouldn't cry or be mad at me. He was extremely composed for an eight year old, reacting well beyond his years. There was no sobbing or screaming, no dropping to the floor or tantrum thrown. As he peered into the box finally realizing the intended joke, he simply said, "That wasn't funny, Grandpa." Fortunately the rest of the morning turned out to be a normal Christmas as the remaining presents brought smiles, hugs, and with time, a perspective that allowed him to laugh about it by the end of the day.

In hindsight this was not my wisest decision or finest attempt at humor. I have shared it though, as it is a valuable reminder of two incredibly important truths that we all must remember as we continue on our path, so that we may experience the fulfilling lives that God has intended for us to live. In the verses above, James highlights what these are.

The first truth is that Our Father who is in heaven, is the same; yesterday, today, and tomorrow. He does not change. Not his character, or righteousness, or faithfulness, or desires, or promises. He loves you, he chose you, and you are his prized possession. Say that out loud a few times throughout your day. **"I am His prized possession!"** He is aware that at some point in all of our lives, we have felt a much greater disappointment than Dylan experienced. It might have been unmet expectations, prayers answered in a way other than you had hoped for, a lost job, a broken relationship or a failure of some sort. Many of these lead to discouragement or depression and are mighty weapons used by Satan in his battle for our hearts. But Paul reminds us who we are in Christ and the hope we can only place in him.

Romans 5:1-5 Therefore, since we have been made right in God's sight by faith, we have peace with God because of what Jesus Christ our Lord has done for us. Because of our faith, Christ has brought us into this place of undeserved privilege where we now stand, and we confidently and joyfully look forward to sharing God's glory. We can rejoice, too, when we run into problems and trials, for we know that they help us develop endurance. And endurance develops strength of character, and character strengthens our confident hope of salvation. **And this hope will not lead to disappointment.** *For we know how dearly God loves us, because he has given us the Holy Spirit to fill our hearts with his love.*

God is the great healer and comforter, the shepherd who protects and watches over his children providing for all of our needs. He has promised to do that. He desires to do that. He knows that you will encounter disappointment and all of the circumstances surrounding it. As you cast all of your worries on him, confident in his love and care for you, he will renew and strengthen you, uplift and guide you through all of life's challenges, bringing praise and glory to his name. Remember these words from David, the man after God's own heart.

Psalms 23 The Lord is my shepherd; I have all that I need. He lets me rest in green meadows; he leads me beside peaceful streams. He renews my strength. He guides me along right paths, bringing honor to his name. Even when I walk through the darkest valley, I will not be afraid, for you are close beside me. Your rod and your staff protect and comfort me. You prepare a feast for me in the presence of my enemies. You honor me by anointing my head with oil. My cup overflows with blessings. Surely your goodness and unfailing love will pursue me all the days of my life, and I will live in the house of the Lord forever.

This passage reassures us that God is always on His Throne; Omniscient, Omnipotent, and Omnipresent. He is fully engaged in your life, and has every possible need or concern already taken care of. Just rest in him. Be renewed by his power. Let him lead, comfort, provide, and protect you for the rest of your days as you bring honor to his name, looking forward with great anticipation to that eternal home that he has been preparing for you. **The contents in God's box will never leave you disappointed**!

The second truth from James is that God is the provider of every good and perfect gift. When we focus inward on our own wants and desires as opposed to what God desires, we will never be satisfied. He knows what is best for each of us. What we need and what we don't. What will bless us and bring glory to him, and what won't. What is eternal and what is temporal. James does not say that God gets it right most of the time or that his gifts are occasionally awesome. He reminds us that they are perfect. **Every gift he gives you is perfect and specifically intended for you.**

I am in awe as I see the evidence of his work all around me and am reminded of who bestows these gifts on us when I sing the powerful hymn, "How Great Thou Art." Carl Boberg, a Swedish pastor, was inspired to write this song while he was traveling in the countryside and was caught in a violent thunderstorm that was followed by clear skies and radiant sunshine, as birds were peacefully chirping in the trees.

> "O Lord my God, when I in awesome wonder, consider all the works thy hands have made. I see the stars, I hear the rolling thunder, Thy power throughout the universe displayed.
>
> When through the woods and forest glades I wander, and hear the birds sing sweetly in the trees. When I look down from lofty mountain grandeur, and hear the brook and feel the gentle breeze.
>
> And when I think that God, his Son not sparing, sent him to die, I scarce can take it in. That on the cross, my burden gladly bearing, he bled and died to take away my sin.
>
> When Christ shall come with shout of acclamation, and take me home, what joy shall fill my heart! Then I shall bow in humble adoration, and there proclaim, My God, how great thou art!
>
> Then sings my soul, my Savior God, to thee: How great thou art! How great thou art! Then sings my soul, my Savior God to thee: How great thou art! How great thou art!"

As you comprehend the magnitude of his greatness, your soul along with all of creation, will sing of his glory now and forever more, joining the praise with the mighty throng of believers who are gathered around his majestic throne.

Brothers and sisters in Christ, we should view every day as Christmas, as God's faithfulness, gifts, and mercies are new each morning, promising us blessings and contentment beyond our comprehension as we love him, love others, and pursue the desires of his heart. As you seek out his treasure and get a glimpse of the contents inside of God's box, unlike Dylan's, they will be greater than you could have ever imagined, you will be thrilled beyond words, more grateful for a gift than ever before, and brought to tears of joy for what you have received. **I hope that when you look at a stick, a rock, and a box in the future, you will remember that you serve a mighty God who has given you every perfect gift, given with the intention to enrich your life and bring glory to his name, and that the plan and path he designed for you will never lead to any disappointment.**

Paul exhorts us to "let our roots grow down into Jesus, and let our lives be built in our Lord, knowing that we are complete through our union with Christ, who is the ruler and authority over all." As you focus your **perspective** on eternity, God's Word, and His people, you will **prioritize** your days accordingly. The talents, passions, and desires that he has gifted to you, when aligned with his plan, will allow you to fulfill that **purpose** which he has called you to pursue, for His Glory.

Number your remaining days wisely.

I pray that God will cover you with his unconditional love, mighty strength, perfect peace, and eternal blessings until the day he calls you home. And while you wait, Wake Up! Run down those stairs to Him with great excitement and anticipation. **Tear open the box that he has prepared - just for you. Give all the glory to him, and enjoy him forever!**

And now, just as you accepted Christ Jesus as your Lord, you must continue to follow him. Let your roots grow down into him, and let your lives be built on him. Then your faith will grow strong in the truth you were taught, and you will overflow with thankfulness. Don't let anyone capture you with empty philosophies and high sounding nonsense that come from human thinking and from spiritual powers of this world, rather than from Christ. For in Christ lives all the fullness of God in a human body. So you also are complete through your union with Christ, who is the head over every ruler and authority.
Colossians 2:6-10

Endnotes

1. Peter Stoner comments on prophecies and odds that they just apply to one man. "Science Speaks" Moody Publishing 1958

2. J. I. Packer, Author of "Knowing God" Inter Varsity Press 1993 "Evidence of spiritual maturity."

3. "In Christ Alone" Keith Getty and Stuart Townend
   Copyright 2002 Thankyou Music (PRS) (adm. Worldwide at CapitolCMGpublishing.com excluding the UK & Europe which is adm. At IntegratedRights.com) All rights reserved. Used by permission.

4. "Bind Us Together" Bob Gillman
   Copyright 1977 Thankyou Music (PRS) (adm. Worldwide at CapitolCMGpublishing.com excluding the UK & Europe which is adm. At IntegratedRights.com) All rights reserved. Used by permission.

5. "Awesome God" Rich Mullins
   Copyright 1988 Universal Music - Brentwood Benson Publ. (ASCAP) (adm. at CapitolCMGPublishing.com) All rights reserved. Used by permission.

6. Dietrich Bonhoeffer German Theologian 1906 - 1946
   "Your life as a Christian should make nonbelievers question their disbelief in God."

7. "Pass It On" Kurt Kaiser
   Copyright 1969 Bud John Songs (ASCAP) (adm.at CapitolCMGPublishing.com) All rights reserved. Used by permission.

8. MLK Jr. "Street Sweeper Quote" from his 1967 speech "What is Your Life's Blueprint"

9. "Because He Lives" Bill and Gloria Gaither
   Copyright 1971 Hanna Street Music (BMI) (adm.at CapitolCMGPublishing.com) All rights reserved. Used by permission.

10. "Thank You" Ray Boltz
    Copyright 1988 Gaither Music Co. (ASCAP) (adm.at CapitolCMGPublishing.com) All rights reserved. Used by permission.

11. "To Obey Is Better Than Sacrifice" Keith Green
    Copyright 1979 Birdwing Music (ASCAP) Ears To Hear Music (ASCAP) Universal Music - Brentwood Benson Publ. (ASCAP) (Adm.at CapitolCMGPublishing.com) All rights reserved. Used by permission.

12. John Driscoll, Reflective Processing Questions "What, So What, Now What" 1994

13. Benjamin Franklin quote "When you fail to plan, you plan to fail"

14. Rafer Johnson 1960 Olympic Decathlon Gold Medalist "Comments on the importance of keeping your goals in sight."

Andy Furman lives in New Braunfels, Texas with his wife Julie and their grandson Dylan. Their 3 grown children live in the area with their families, including 4 additional grandchildren. Andy and Julie have been involved in camping and church ministries for 40 years, as well as facilitating team building and developmental leadership experiences.

Made in the USA
Middletown, DE
16 February 2022

61186690R00066